Nick Barber's ENGLISH SELECTION

95 tunes with chords, from English traditional music sessions
Suitable for all melody instruments

Nick Barber's English Choice

Since 2002 *Nick Barber's English Choice* has been turning up on pub tables wherever English traditional music is being played. This Mally Production, affectionately referred to as "The Red Book", has proved very popular, and many musicians have asked "When is the next volume coming out?" Well, here it is! The BLUE Book. *Nick Barber's English Choice*, and accompanying CDs *Bonny Kate* (DMPCD0203) and *Lovely Nancy* (DMPCD0204), are still available from traditional music shops or direct from the publishers.

Recordings

This book is complemented by two excellent soundtracks, *Oldham Rant* (DMPCD1105) and *Grand Chain* (DMPCD1104). The two soundtracks of all the tunes in the book have been specially recorded by Nick, playing his D/G Loffet melodeon, horn and soprano recorder. Nick's wife Mary assisted by recording some of the tracks on fiddle. The recordings are available from traditional music shops or direct from the publishers.

Nick Barber's ENGLISH SELECTION

Acknowledgements

For permission to use their compositions I would like to thank the following:
- Flos Headford for *Prince Albert's Jig*
- Simon Ritchie for *The Valiant*
- Frederick Paris and his publisher Philippe Besson (Parsiparla) for *Jour d'Été*
- Cliff Stapleton for *Poolside Polka*
- Will Hampson for *Bus Stop*
- Bernice Harding for permission to use Jim Harding's *South Downs*
- Keld Norgaard Kristensen for *Reggish*

Thanks are due to Bruce Baillie for the chapter headings.
Thanks to Diane Richardson for the session photographs.

Nick Barber's English Selection   Compiled and arranged by Nick Barber

Tune arrangements, harmonies and text copyright © Nick Barber 2011

ISBN 978 1 899512 77 5

A catalogue in print record for this title is available from the British Library.

Rear cover photo of Nick: Mary Barber
Cover instrument collage: James Noon at Chameleon Design   Telephone: 01484 304545
Original cover design: Bryan Ledgard at Ledgard Jepson Ltd.   Telephone 01226 766608

All rights reserved. No part of this book may be reproduced in any form whatsoever without prior written permission from the publisher, except for short extracts for reviews. This book is sold subject to the condition that it shall not, by way of trade or otherwise, be lent, re-sold or otherwise circulated without the publisher's prior consent, in any form of binding or cover other than that in which it is published.

It is illegal to photocopy any part of this book

Produced and published by **mally.com**
3 East View, Moorside, Cleckheaton, West Yorkshire, BD19 6LD, U.K.
Tel: +44 (0)1274 876388   Fax: +44 (0)1274 865208
Email: mally@mally.com   Web: http://www.mally.com
Copyright © 2011 mally

A mally production

Foreword by Flos Headford

Nick and Mary Barber are familiar faces to all the regular attenders at the famous Radway musicians' sessions at Sidmouth festival. At these gatherings, they are an inspiration to one and all, their infectious enthusiasm (and apparently boundless stamina) providing a superb example of the kind of devotion that English music can engender. For many years they also provided direct instruction with the Big Band (for learners) at the same festival.

If you want a good example of how English music ought to be played, you can do little better than obtain a copy of the "Four Across" CD, by the band English Rebellion, where they are joined by Mary Humphreys and Anahata.

Nick has already produced a collection of tunes played in sessions, English Choice, which is regarded by many as an essential handbook, and is certainly handy to know about when a beginner asks "Where can I find some of these lovely tunes?"

With that in mind, you can rest assured of the wisdom in buying this present book. I wish you all joy as you learn and play the music here.

Flos (Phil) Headford, Old Swan Band 11th April 2011

Nick Barber's ENGLISH SELECTION

Nick Barber

Nick Barber plays melodeon, horn, baritone and recorder in the ceilidh band English Rebellion and is musician for the West Yorkshire Cotswold morris side, White Rose. The baritone also gets outings with North Yorkshire band, the Village Hop Band, and the Lofthouse and Middlesmoor Silver Band – whilst the horn gets its turn with the Huddersfield Philharmonic Orchestra and Orchestra of Square Chapel.

His previous publication, Nick Barber's English Choice, is also available from Mally productions. Matching CDs are available for both books.

With his wife Mary (fiddle), Nick released the CD Crossword in 1997, and in 2009 recorded the CD Four Across with English Rebellion, on the WildGoose label.

Session at the Tap and Spile, Harrogate

Nick Barber's English Selection

Contents

Aperitif
		Page No.
1.	The Cream Pot	5
2.	Bang Upp	6
3.	Cotillion	6
4.	Sally Sloane's Jig	7
5.	The Feathers	7
6.	Lord Zouch's Maske	8
7.	Angela Mary Lee	8
8.	Chelsea Reach	8
9.	Chelmsford Assembly	9
10.	The Honeymoon	9
11.	Oldham Rant	9
12.	Spanish Patriots	10
13.	Duke of York's Hornpipe	10
14.	Cuckolds All a Row	11
15.	Grimstock	11
16.	Lady's Plaything	11
17.	Red Lion	12
18.	Tumblers Hornpipe	12
19.	Lilly Lips	12
20.	Hudane	12
21.	London Hornpipe	13
22.	Stony Steps	13

Starters
23.	Fête du Village	14
24.	Mittell's Hornpipe	14
25.	The Quarryman	15
26.	Lemonville Jig	15
27.	Uncle Jim's	16
28.	Prince Albert's Jig	16
29.	Soldiers' Joy (Suffolk)	17
30.	Three Jolly Sheepskins	17
31.	Butcher's Hornpipe	17
32.	Sadlers Wells	18
33.	Coleford Jig	18
34.	Albert Farmer's Bonfire Tune	18
35.	Watson's Hornpipe	19
36.	Grand Chain	19
37.	Hill's Fancy	20
38.	Double Figure Eight	20
39.	Will's Way	21
40.	Sweeps Hornpipe	21
41.	Tom Tolley's Hornpipe	21
42.	Little Burnt Potato	22
43.	Basquet of Oysters	22

Main Course
44.	The Valiant	23
45.	Tyskeren	23
46.	Poolside Polka	24
47.	Dennington Bell	24
48.	Bath Hornpipe	25
49.	Cook Hornpipe	25
50.	Cuckoo's Nest	25
51.	Miss Gayton's Hornpipe	26
52.	Miss Menager's Hornpipe	26
53.	Holywell Hornpipe	26
54.	Officer's Polka	27
55.	Mr Rew's Polka	27
56.	Clee Hill	27
57.	Roman Wall	28
58.	East Bolden	28
59.	Ann Frazer McKenzie	29
60.	Duke of York's Quickstep	29
61.	Boys of School Hill	29
62.	Mount Hills	30
63.	Maiden Lane	30
64.	Bus Stop	30
65.	Kurakin	30
66.	Rosalie Prairie Flower	31
67.	Kirkgate Hornpipe	31
68.	March in Bluebeard	31
69.	Shropshire Lass	32
70.	LNB Polka	32
71.	Radstock Jig	32
72.	Leeds Polka	33
73.	Grand Hornpipe	33
74.	Fourpence Halfpenny Farthing	33
75.	The Flight	34
76.	The Ball	34
77.	Bellingham Boat	34

Dessert
78.	Draper's Maggot	35
79.	Bloomsbury Market	35
80.	Robertson's Hornpipe	36
81.	The Plane Tree	36
82.	Said Too Much Already	36
83.	Cumberland Waltz	36
84.	L'Inconnue de Limoise	37
85.	The Leaving of Lismore	37
86.	Jour d'Été	37
87.	Westmorland	38
88.	Hole in the Wall	38
89.	French Waltz	38
90.	In the Toyshop	39
91.	Mick's Tune	39
92.	South Downs	39
93.	Reggish	40
94.	Never Again	40
95.	Les Filles de mon Pays	40

Introduction
Nick Barber's ENGLISH SELECTION

This book was compiled for musicians who, though competent on their instrument, would like some help getting involved in the English folk session scene. It follows on from a previous Mally publication, Nick Barber's English Choice.

A music session is like a conversation, and in order to take part you need certain basic tools. If you're going to join in with the tunes you hear being played, you need to know which tunes to expect. And if you plan to learn these tunes, you will probably find a printed version of the tune useful. If you plan to start a set of tunes during a session, you need to know which tunes other musicians would be likely to know and join in with. This book aims to present a selection of tunes for this purpose.

Because there is an element of fashion in the repertoire of any session, I have tried to select tunes which have been around for years, and which no doubt will still be played for years to come. Wherever possible I have noted the sources of the tunes. If you like a particular tune, I would urge you to pursue it a little and go to the source, whether this is a manuscript, a published book, a recording or a real live musician. In the words of Barry Callaghan, "Tunes...have a life story, and have participated in the life stories of the countless musicians who have played them...they all come trailing their history." He goes on to encourage us to "look for the life stories as we meet further tunes".

You will notice that I have included a few tunes of French and Danish origin – these tunes have been taken on board by English session players, and are played in an English style.

I would not advise you to take this book along to a session. You'll get beer on the nice shiny cover. And it's quite hard to locate a tune fast enough to make use of the book. And the version you hear won't be the same as the one printed. And anyway, it's more important to listen, and respond to what you hear, than it is to play exactly the "right" notes. Better would be to use the book later, to remember some of the things you heard, and to try out some new ones.

I've organised the book in a slightly unusual way – its structure follows the structure of a typical session. First there's the opening phase (I've called it the Aperitif) where things are quiet...people are still arriving, there's plenty of space, and players don't yet know each other very well. Contributions to the session at this stage are likely to remain as solos – people are more likely to listen and enjoy your playing. The tunes in the book reflect this – although still standard English session repertoire, they're a little more special and unusual than some of the later choices. The second phase of the session (I've called this Starters) is a sort of pulling-in process, where the tunes chosen have the aim of getting everyone started. They are the best-known tunes, for everyone to warm up on. Thirdly we have the Main Course tunes. The session is in full swing, and the tunes in this section are the loudest and the liveliest. Finally, there is often a winding-down process (Dessert). Maybe because it's getting late and someone's asleep upstairs, maybe for other reasons...the last tunes in the book are more reflective, gentle tunes to finish off with.

Within each section the order of the tunes has no special significance. I've put tunes near each other which can be played together – as on the accompanying CD. But you should do your own experiments as to which tune you would like to play with which other.

The music notation is a representation of what I actually play – this is normally close to what will be found in the quoted sources, but in several places I have preferred a "session version". The chords indicated are roughly the ones I would play on the melodeon.

There are a few things you should bear in mind if you're new to sessions:

Notice who started playing a set of tunes. They may well want to lead the session into a second tune, usually after the first tune has been played about three times. Similarly, when the time comes to finish, it's up to that person to indicate this. Don't feel that there has to be a rule about the number of times tunes are played. Some sessions have expectations, others don't. Sometimes is good to play a single tune many times through – giving it time to really develop and take off.

If you want to start a set of tunes yourself, make sure that it's one you're comfortable playing, and if there's a second tune be sure that you can get into it from the first tune without breaking down. Be wary of playing too fast...it's easy to do so when you're tense. In most sessions you don't need to wait to be asked to play – just wait for a suitable lull in the proceedings.

Don't compete. If someone's playing too loud or too fast, you won't improve things by starting a musical battle. And don't string together an endless succession of tunes – there are other people in the room!!

Finally – ENJOY YOUR PLAYING!!

1. *Oldham Rant Track 1a*   ***The Cream Pot***

THE CREAM POT occurs in the William Vickers manuscript of 1770 and was published in *Aird's Airs* in 1782. It was commonly known as **The Kern Staff**.

Aird's Airs
Published in six volumes between 1778 and 1801, and edited and published in Glasgow by J. A. Aird, the *Selection of Scotch, English, Irish and Foreign Airs* has long been a source of tunes for English musicians. Many tunes have found their way from Aird's collections into musicians' manuscript tunebooks. Volumes 1-3 are available online via Richard Robinson's website. This website is a good resource for anyone interested in traditional music (see http://richardrobinson.tunebook.org.uk). Jack Campin's web page (see http://www.campin.me.uk) is also well worth a visit - he has published all 6 volumes of *Aird's Airs* online. Web addresses correct in April 2011.

Bang Upp

Oldham Rant Track 1b **2.**

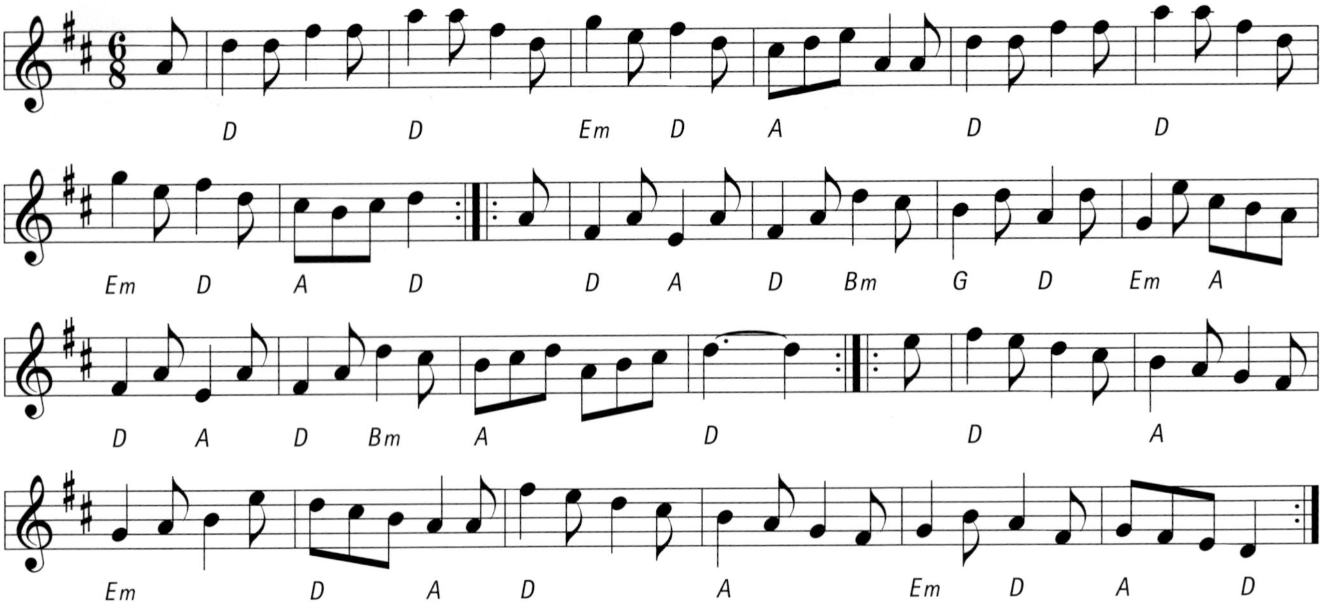
D D Em D A D D
Em D A D D A D Bm G D Em A
D A D Bm A D D A
Em D A D A Em D A D

BANG UPP is to be found in William Docker's manuscript and other sources.

COTILLION has been popularised in *Lewes Favourites*, the tune book of the Lewes Arms Folk Club. The tune is from the nineteenth-century manuscript of the Bosham Band, Sussex.

Cotillion

Oldham Rant Track 2a **3.**

G G D G D D C D G G D C G
G G C G G Bm Am G
D D C D G G D C G

Session at the Radway, Sidmouth

4. Oldham Rant Track 3a

Sally Sloane's Jig

A version of SALLY SLOANE'S JIG is to be found in the Lawrence Leadley manuscript as **The Trip to Cottingham**. The tune has travelled - this version is from the Australian melodeon player, fiddler and singer, Sally Sloane, who died in 1982.

There are a few sources for THE FEATHERS. This version, with its unusual G minor third part, is to be found in Broderip's *Playing the Harpsichord, Spinnet or Pianoforte Made Easy by New Instructions*, in the Vaughan Williams Memorial Library.

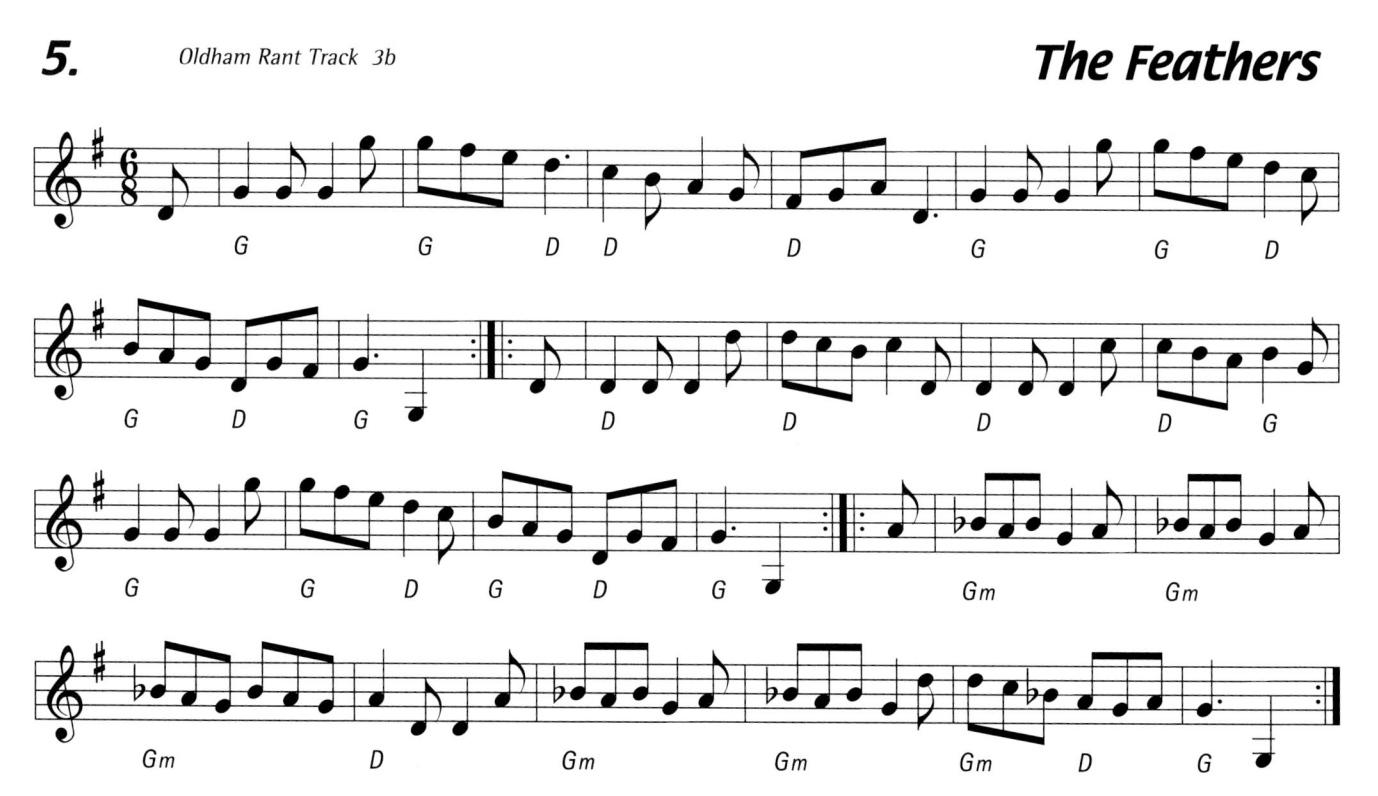

5. Oldham Rant Track 3b

The Feathers

Sally Sloane
Sally Sloane (1894-1982) is a legendary figure in the world of Australian traditional song. Though a player of accordion, button accordion, fiddle, mouth organ and piano, she is remembered primarily as a singer. She learned most of her songs from her mother, who in turn learned them from her own mother. She was recorded extensively by John Meredith, producing a large collection of songs and dance tunes.

6. Lord Zouch's Maske
Oldham Rant Track 2b

7. Angela Mary Lee
Oldham Rant Track 4

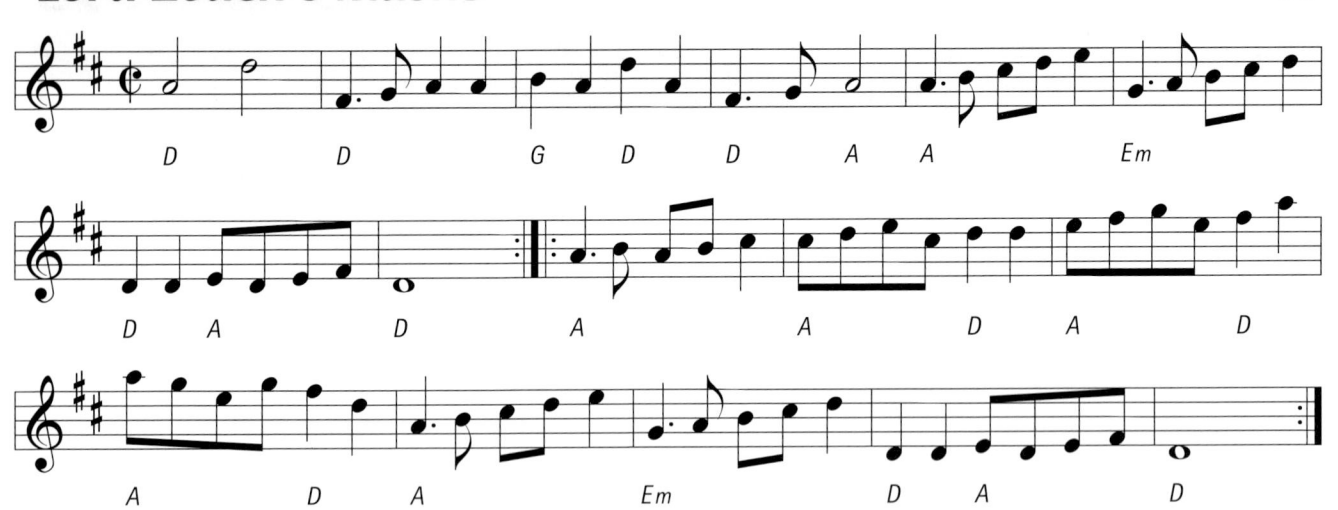

8. Chelsea Reach
Oldham Rant Track 5a

LORD ZOUCHE'S MASKE is an Elizabethan tune attributed to the English lutenist and composer John Johnson. Maskes were a lavish courtly version of the mummers' plays, and included dance, music, song and poetry. Leading dramatists and composers were employed to write them - and elements of the maske can be seen in Shakespeare's plays, eg A Midsummer Night's Dream.

ANGELA MARY LEE was written by Nick Barber in memory of Angela, who died tragically in 2009. She was well-known in the North of England as a dancer, musician and artist.

CHELSEA REACH is from Playford's *Dancing Master*. Jeremy Barlow's complete edition is well worth getting hold of - a great source of tunes.

9. *Oldham Rant Track 5b*

Chelmsford Assembly

10. *Oldham Rant Track 6a*

The Honeymoon

11. *Oldham Rant Track 6b*

Oldham Rant

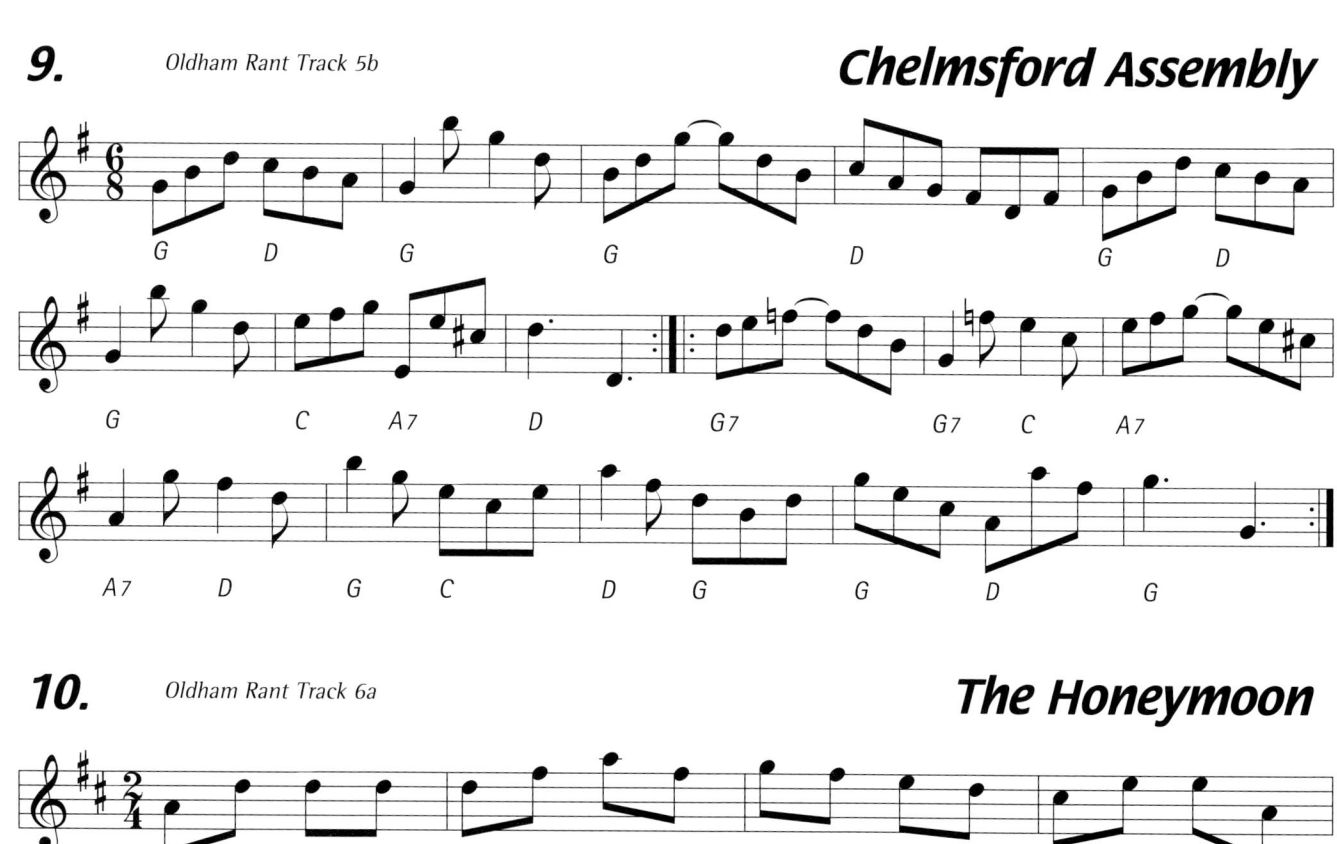

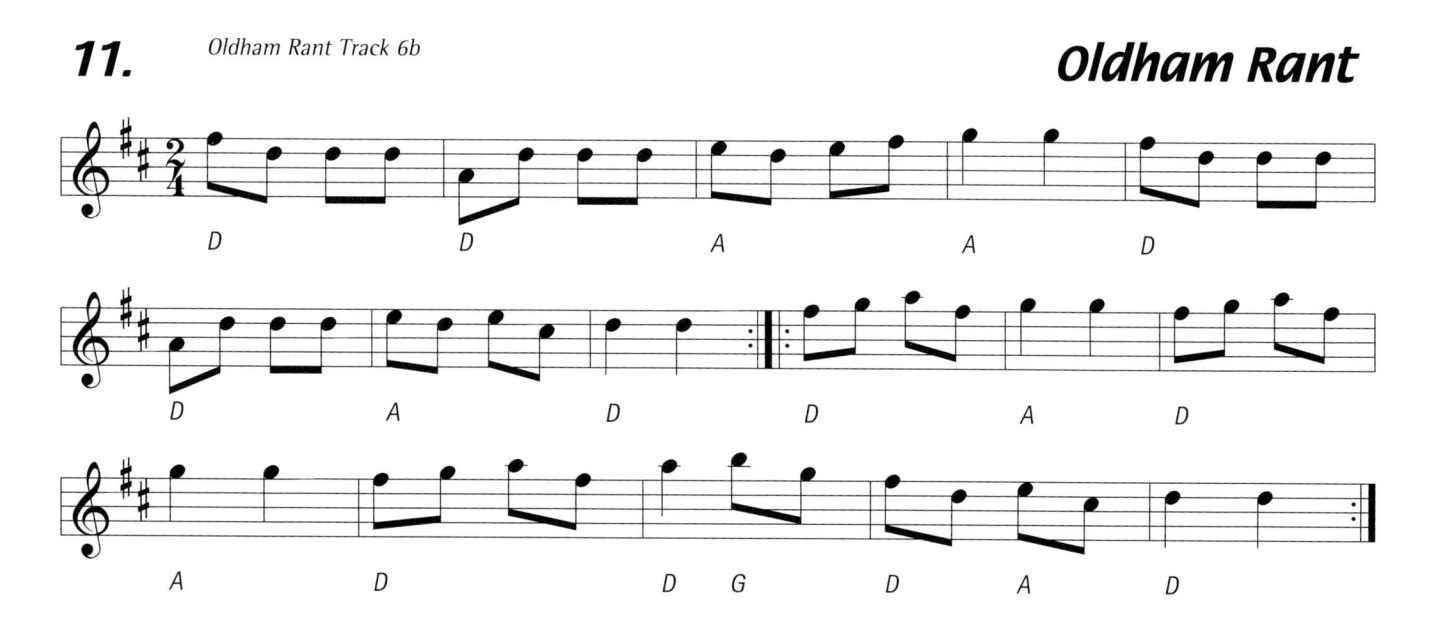

CHELMSFORD ASSEMBLY is another tune from Playford's *Dancing Master*.

THE HONEYMOON, together with OLDHAM RANT, are great session tunes - simple enough to pick up by ear quite quickly, but with plenty of rhythmic drive.

You can play OLDHAM RANT at the same time as THE HONEYMOON - they fit together perfectly. In a session, watch out - it's quite likely that someone will think you were playing *Shepherd's Hey* and start playing that instead.

Nick Barber's English Selection

Spanish Patriots

Oldham Rant Track 7a **12.**

D D Em D A D
D Em D D D Em A
D A D Em A D A D

The title SPANISH PATRIOTS could refer to the Spanish patriots who were resisting French occupation in around 1810. Thomas Stott wrote:

"The thundering tide of red-wing'd vengeance pour
Upon the proud oppressor's guilty head,
Whom abject Europe now beholds with dread."

Duke of York's Hornpipe

Oldham Rant Track 7b **13.**

D A D A A D
A D A D D Em
A D D A D A D

DUKE OF YORK'S HORNPIPE like SPANISH PATRIOTS can be found in the Lawrence Leadley manuscript. Both tunes can be played at quite a steady pace.

Session at Holmfirth Festival

14. Cuckolds All a Row
Oldham Rant Track 8b

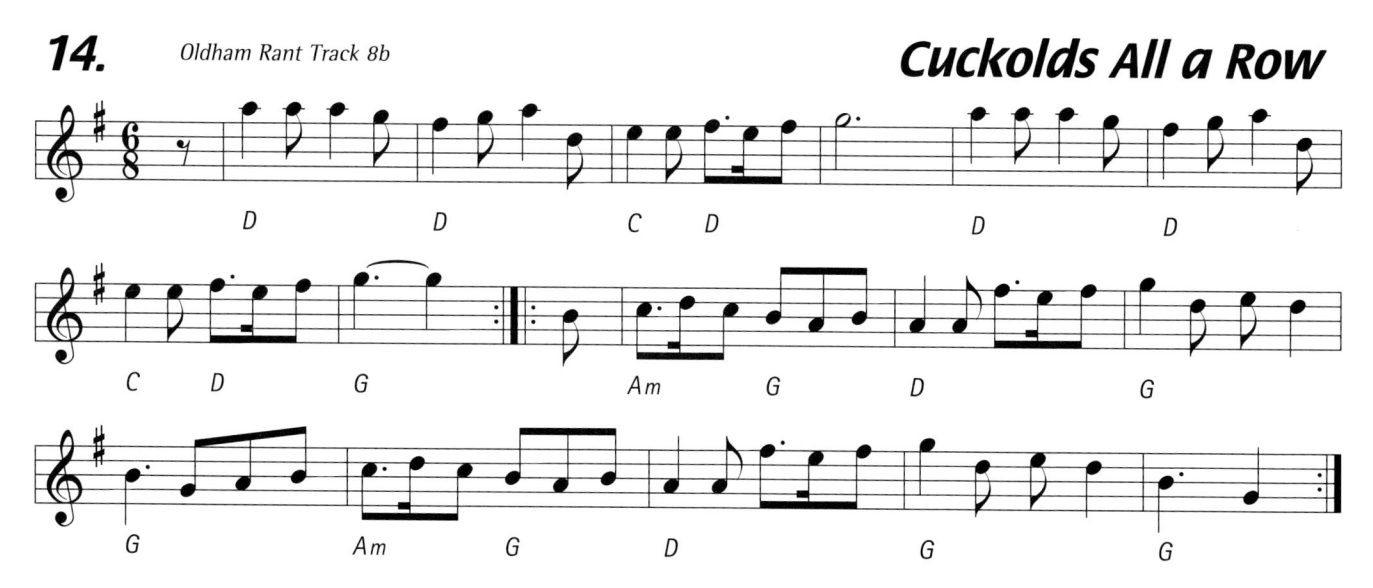

Jeremy Barlow, in his complete edition of the Playford Tunes, uses this tune to show the changes through the book's 18 editions, neatly illustrating how musical notation changed between 1651 and 1701.

There is nothing 'grim' about GRIMSTOCK. The B strain might sound over-repetitive at first, but the more you play it the more you will enjoy it!

LADY'S PLAYTHING is also known as **General Howe's March**. This tune can be found in the 1798 manuscript of Joshua Jackson.

15. Grimstock
Oldham Rant Track 8a

16. Lady's Plaything
Oldham Rant Track 8c

Nick Barber's English Selection

Red Lion

Oldham Rant Track 9a **17.**

(Sheet music in 3/2, key of D major)
Chords: D A D D A D D A A D A D
D A D G D D A D A D

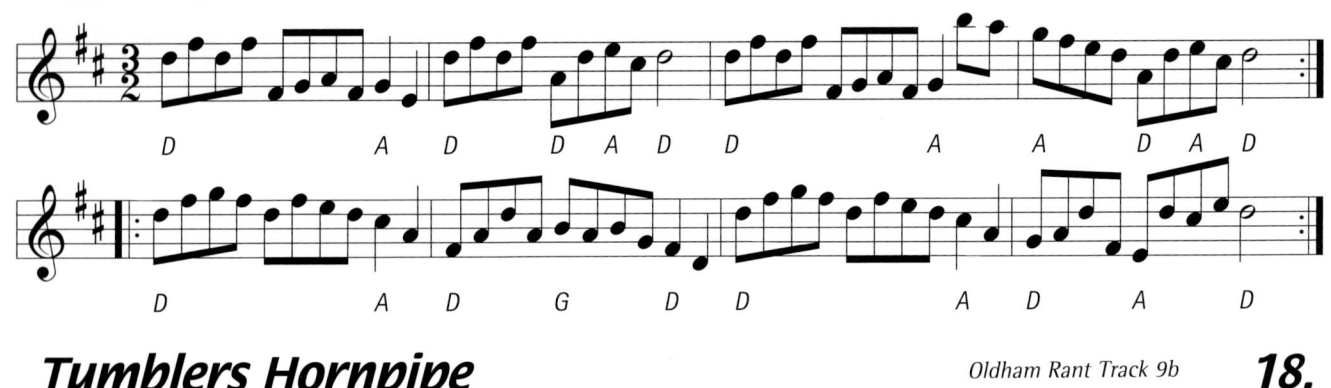

Tumblers Hornpipe

Oldham Rant Track 9b **18.**

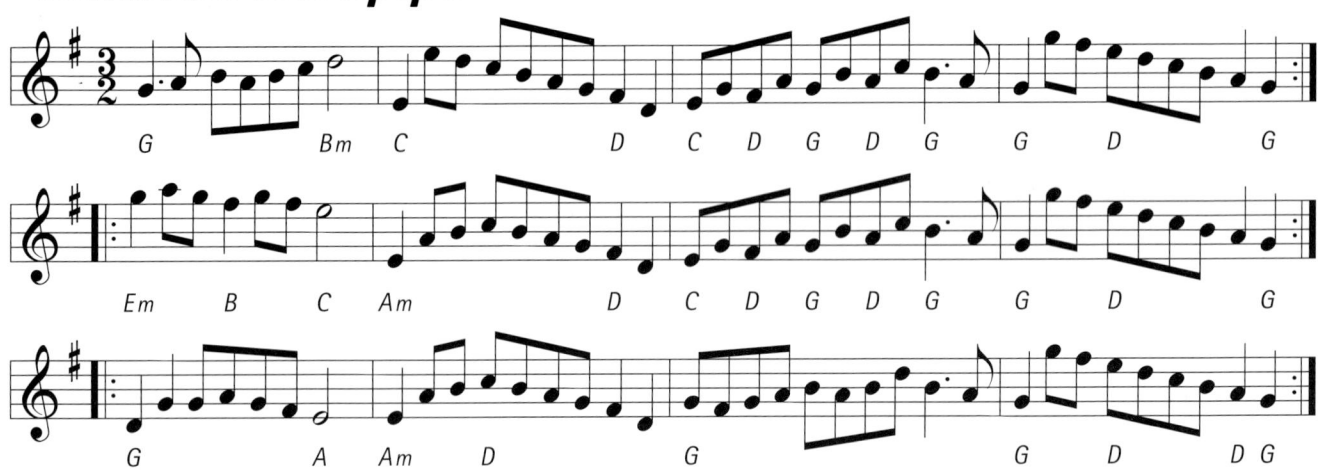

(Sheet music in 3/2, key of G major)
Chords: G Bm C D C D G D G G D G
Em B C Am D C D G D G G D G
G A Am D G G D D G

Lilly Lips

Oldham Rant Track 10a **19.**

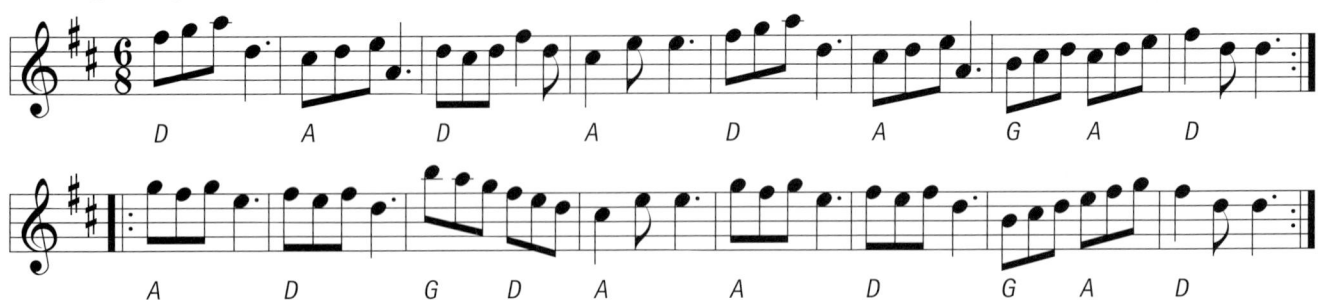

(Sheet music in 6/8, key of D major)
Chords: D A D A D A G A D
A D G D A A D G A D

Hudane

Oldham Rant Track 10b **20.**

(Sheet music in 6/8, key of D major)
Chords: D G D A A D G D
Em A A D A Bm D A
A A Bm D A A

RED LION is one of the better known examples of the triple-time hornpipe. In the words of John Offord, "The 3/2 hornpipes offer a supreme addition to the repertoire and many fine fiddlers in the revival are beginning to realise this."
TUMBLERS HORNPIPE is to be found in a manuscript entitled *James Biggins - his book* in Leeds reference library.
LILLY LIPS is a rattling good jig from the early nineteenth-century publishers Button and Whitaker.
HUDANE is from Hodsdull's *24 Favourite Country Dances for the year 1826*.

21. London Hornpipe
Oldham Rant Track 11a

LONDON HORNPIPE is one of the most popular hornpipes from the Lawrence Leadley manuscript.

There are many different versions of STONY STEPS. The one reproduced here is from Wilson's *Companion to the Ballroom* (1816).

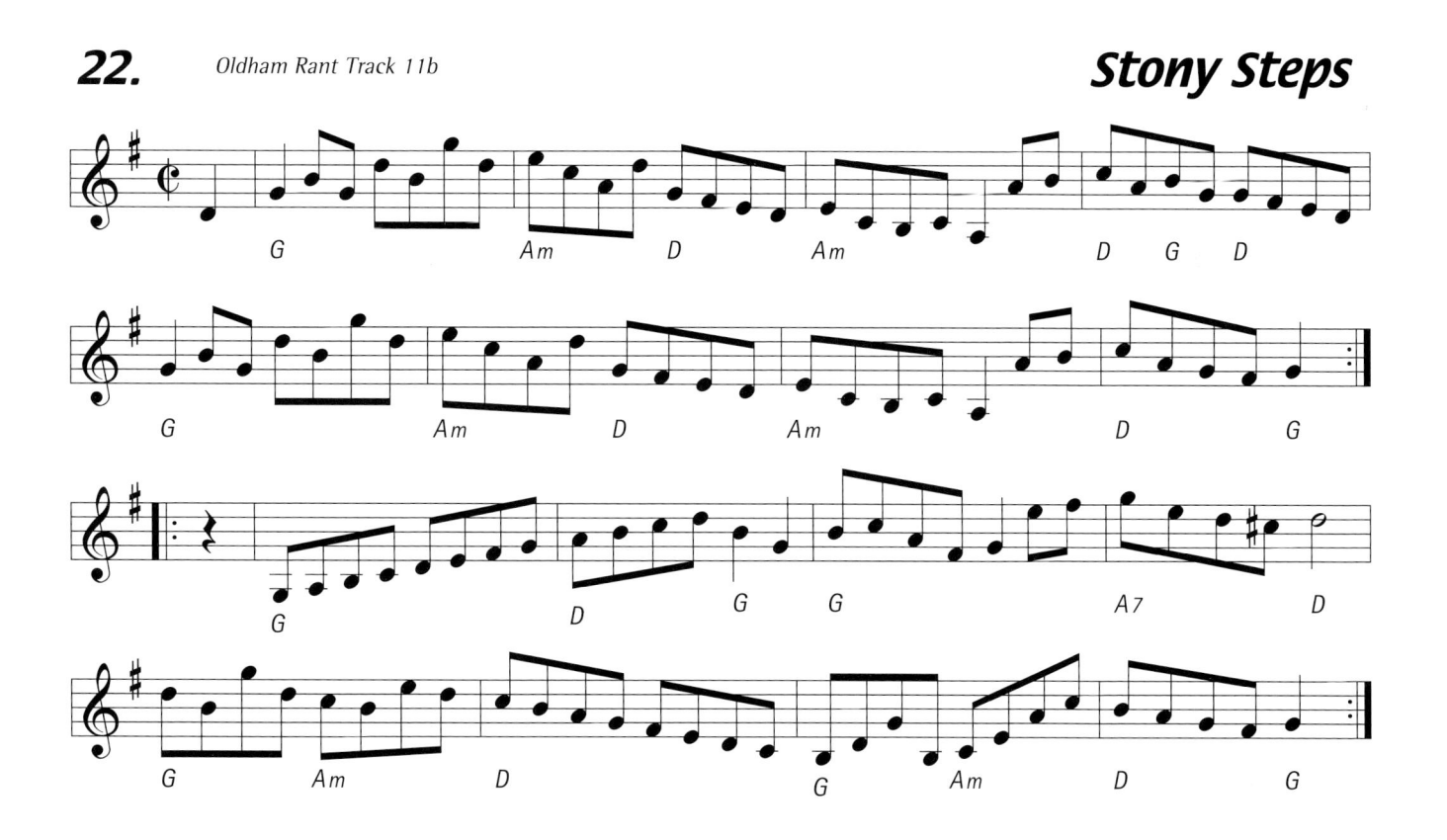

22. Stony Steps
Oldham Rant Track 11b

Triple Time Hornpipes and John Offord

John Offord's little book *John of the Greeny Cheshire Way* has been very influential in the promotion of triple-time hornpipes, probably originating from Lancashire and Cheshire. A new edition - *John of the Green - The Cheshire Way* is a much expanded collection, bringing back to life what was once a very popular and widespread musical form, which is now sadly neglected.

STARTERS

Fête du Village

Grand Chain Track 1a **23.**

FÊTE DU VILLAGE is a session player's favourite. This tune is from *William Mittell, His Book.* It can be played briskly, or in quite a slow and dreamy fashion.

MITTELL'S HORNPIPE is simply entitled "**Hornpipe**" in Mittell's book.

Mittell's Hornpipe

Grand Chain Track 1b **24.**

Nick Barber's English Selection

25. The Quarryman
Grand Chain Track 2a — Written by Charlie Sherritt

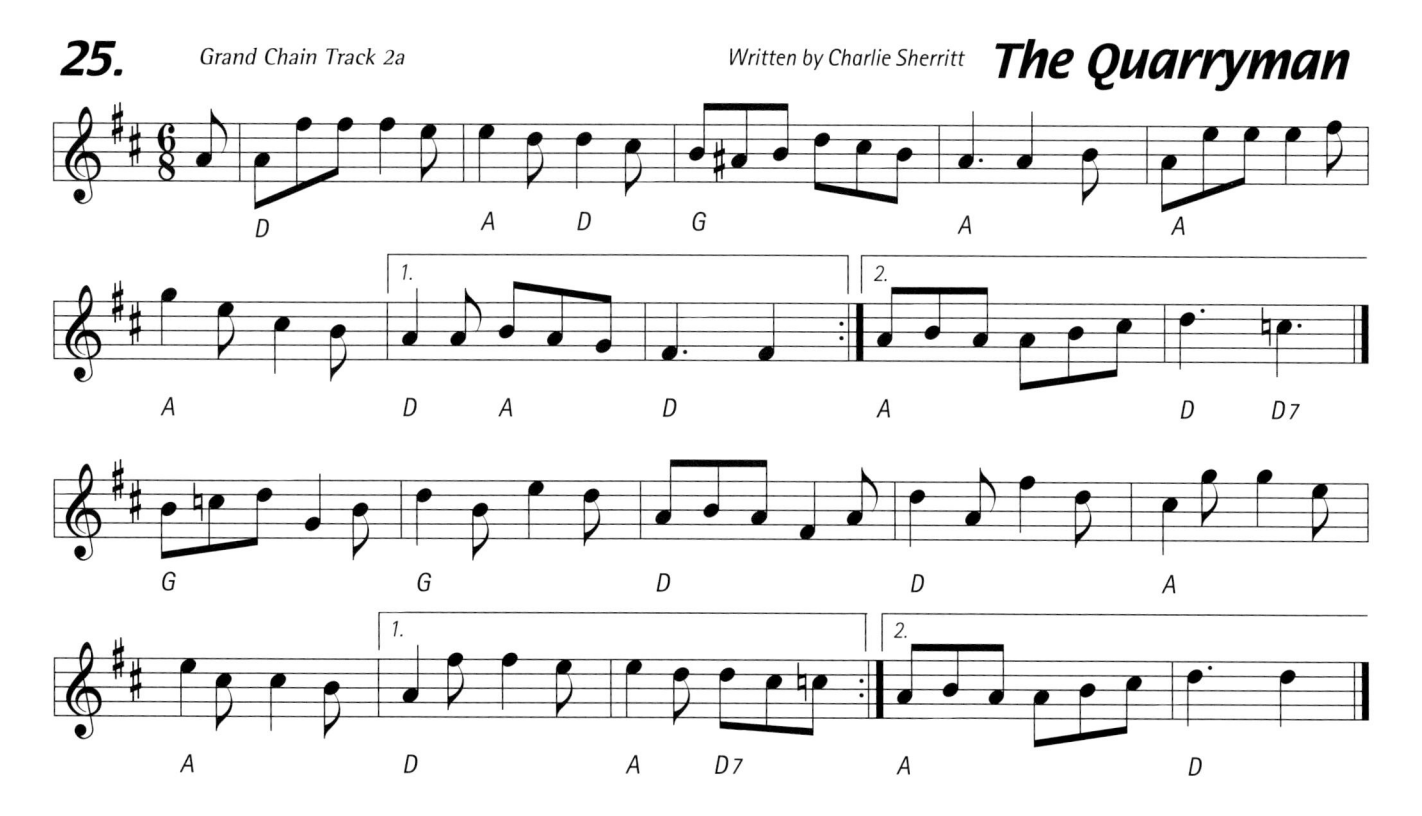

THE QUARRYMAN comes from the playing of Willie Taylor, and was written by Charlie Sherritt.

LEMONVILLE JIG is, again, from the playing of Willie Taylor, and written by Canadian, Jack Hayes.

26. Lemonville Jig
Grand Chain Track 2b — Written by Jack Hayes

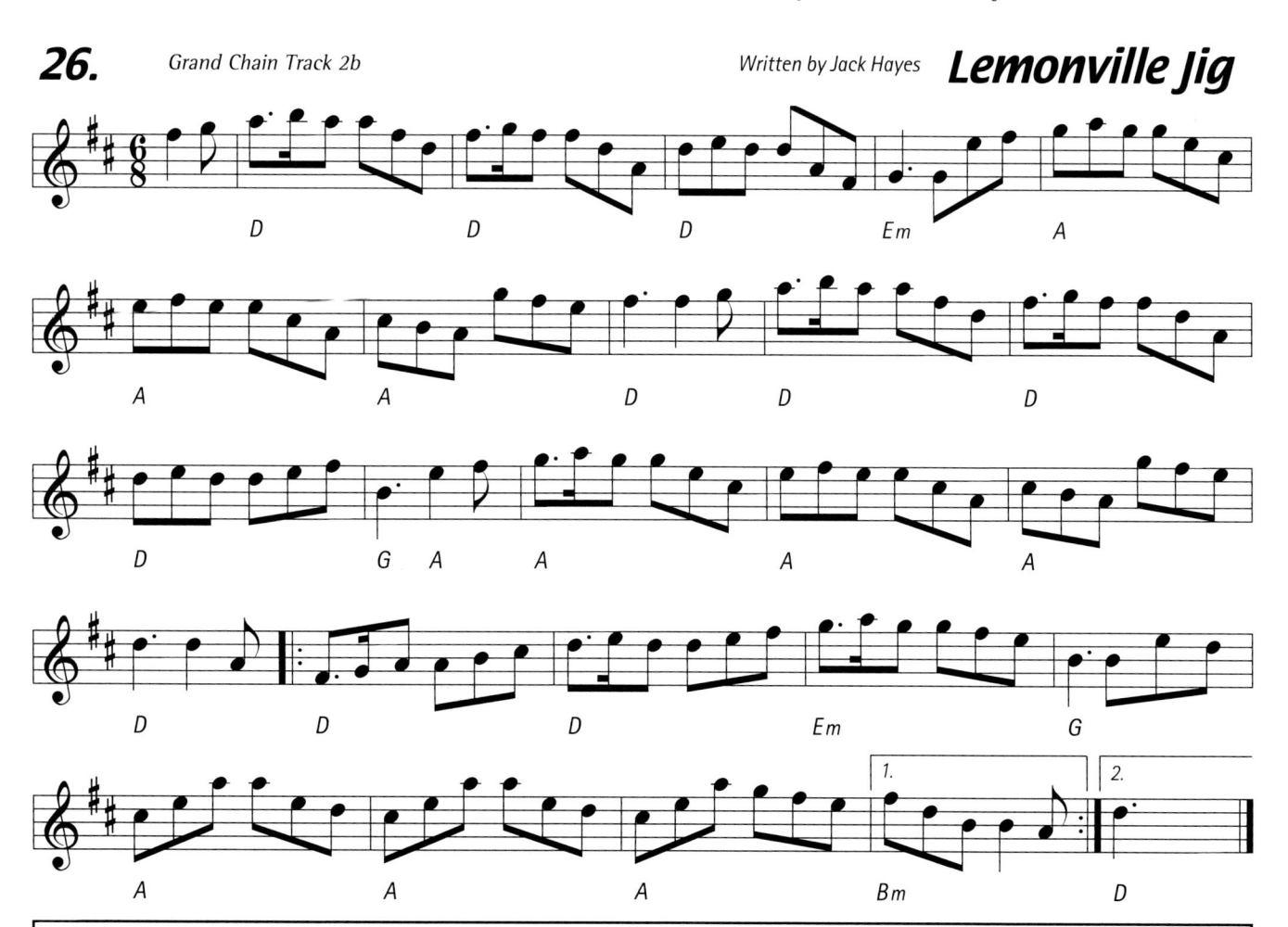

Willie Taylor and The Shepherds
Northumbrian fiddler Willie Taylor, with Will Atkinson (mouth organ) and Joe Hutton (pipes), became well known as The Shepherds. Willie Taylor's fiddle style has been described as "quintessentially Northumbrian" and you can hear all three players by visiting the FARNE website (see page 28).

Nick Barber's English Selection

Uncle Jim's

Grand Chain Track 3a — **27.**

UNCLE JIM'S is from the playing of Bob Cann - you can hear recordings of Bob's playing on a CD released on the Veteran label: "Proper Job", Bob Cann.

PRINCE ALBERT'S JIG was composed by Flos Headford in honour of the wonderful sessions at the Prince Albert, Rodborough Hill, Stroud.

Prince Albert's Jig

Written by Flos Headford Grand Chain Track 3b — **28.**

Nick Barber's English Selection

29. Soldiers' Joy (Suffolk)
Grand Chain Track 4a

30. Three Jolly Sheepskins
Grand Chain Track 4b

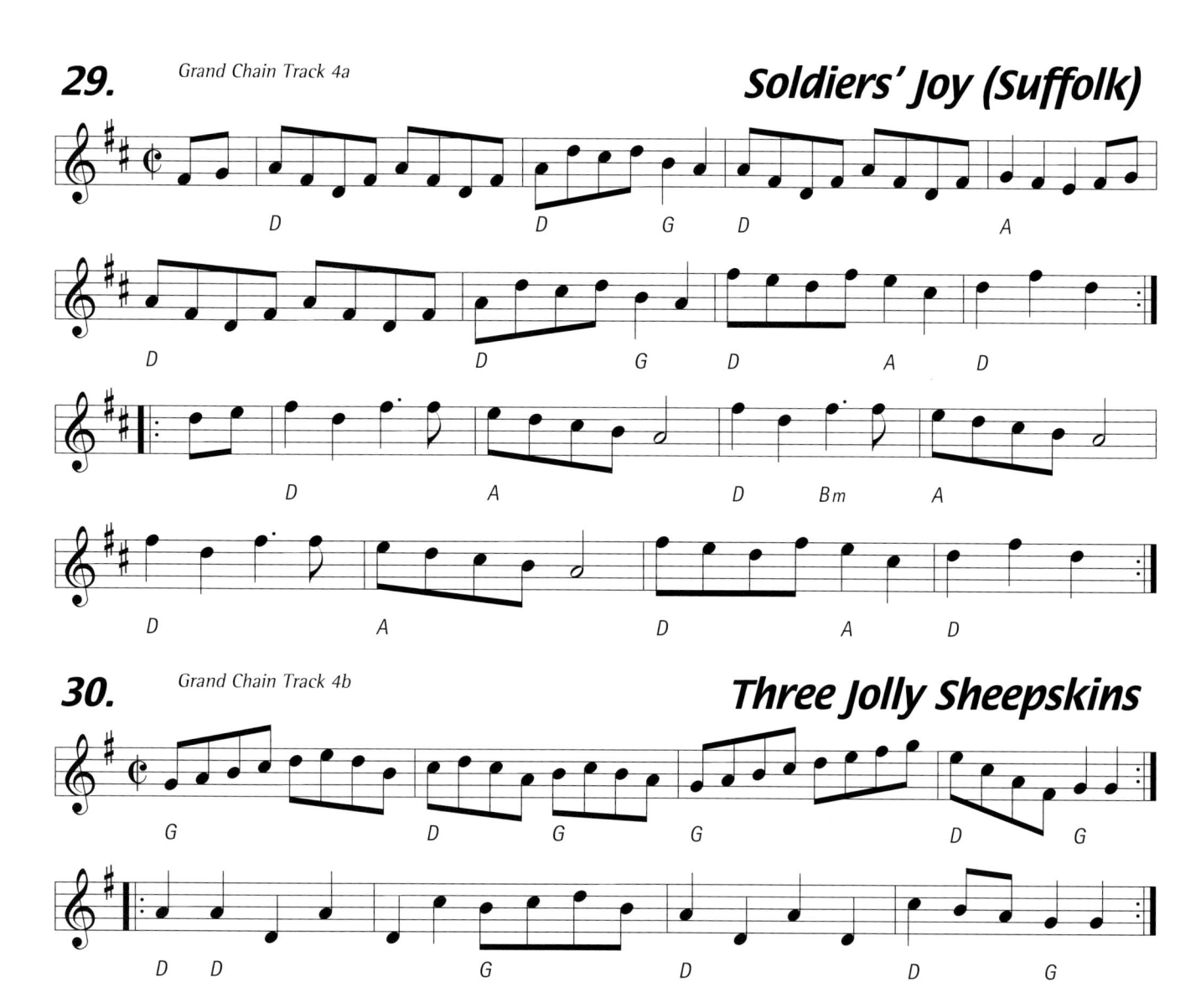

SOLDIERS' JOY is one of the most enduringly popular tunes. This version comes from Suffolk.

THREE JOLLY SHEEPSKINS is a sword dance tune recorded in 1909 by Cecil Sharp, using the latest technology - a wax cylinder. The musician on that occasion was John Locke of Leominster.

BUTCHER'S HORNPIPE is a favourite with fiddle players, though the range of the notes makes it awkward or unplayable on some instruments. You may need to play the first eleven notes in a higher octave.

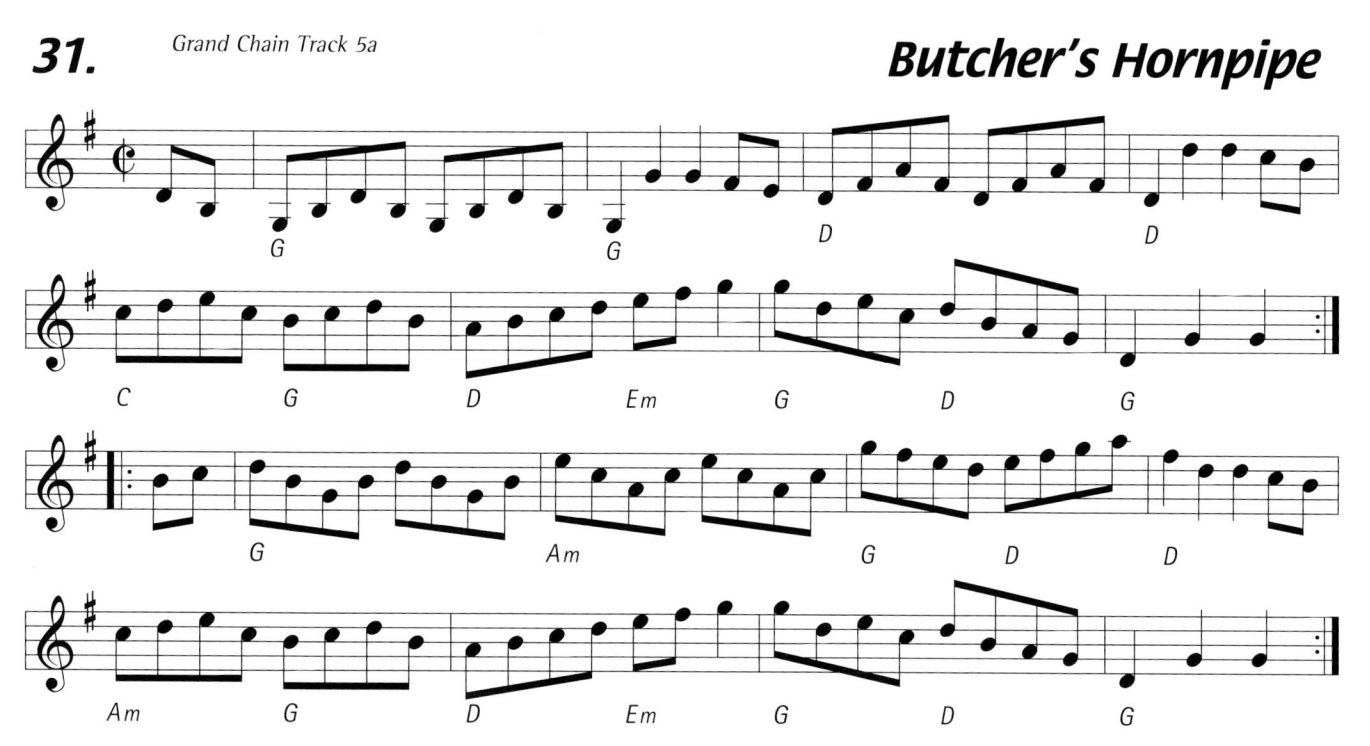

31. Butcher's Hornpipe
Grand Chain Track 5a

Sadlers Wells

Grand Chain Track 5b — **32.**

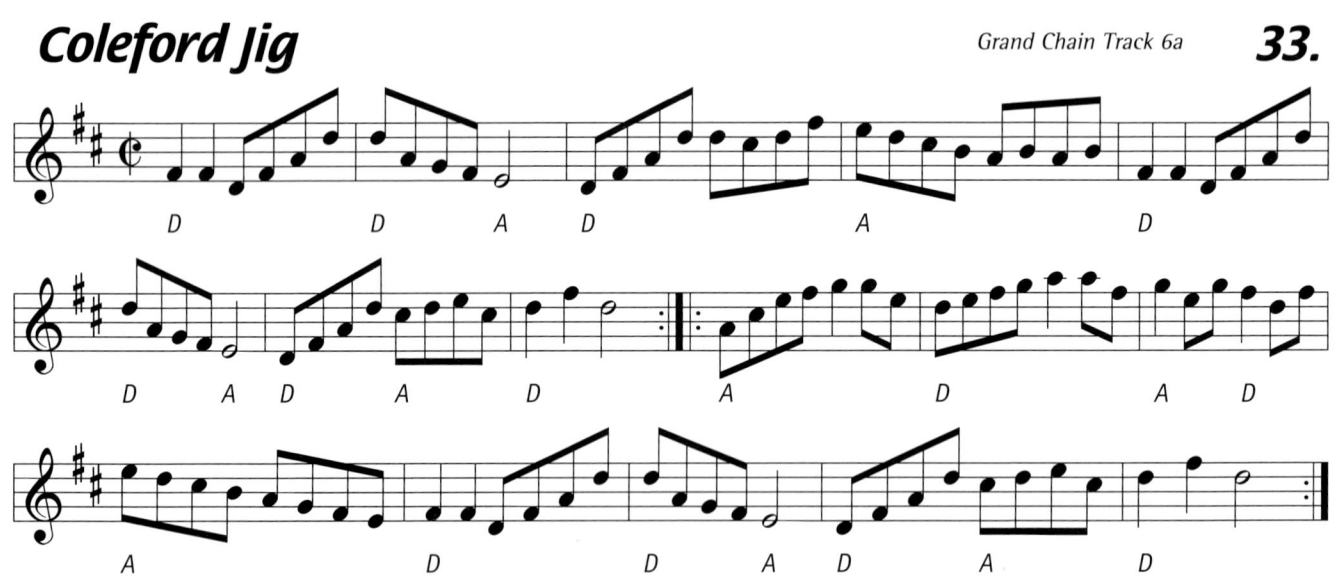

Coleford Jig

Grand Chain Track 6a — **33.**

SADLERS WELLS is another good fiddle tune, and again you may need to adjust the notes a little - but it's worth it!
COLEFORD JIG is from the playing of Gloucestershire fiddler Stephen Baldwin, and is not a jig. But as Stephen Baldwin said, "It's a bit of a job to know all them names!".
ALBERT FARMER'S BONFIRE TUNE started to get known as a session tune after it was recorded by The Bismarcks on *Upstream* in 2001.

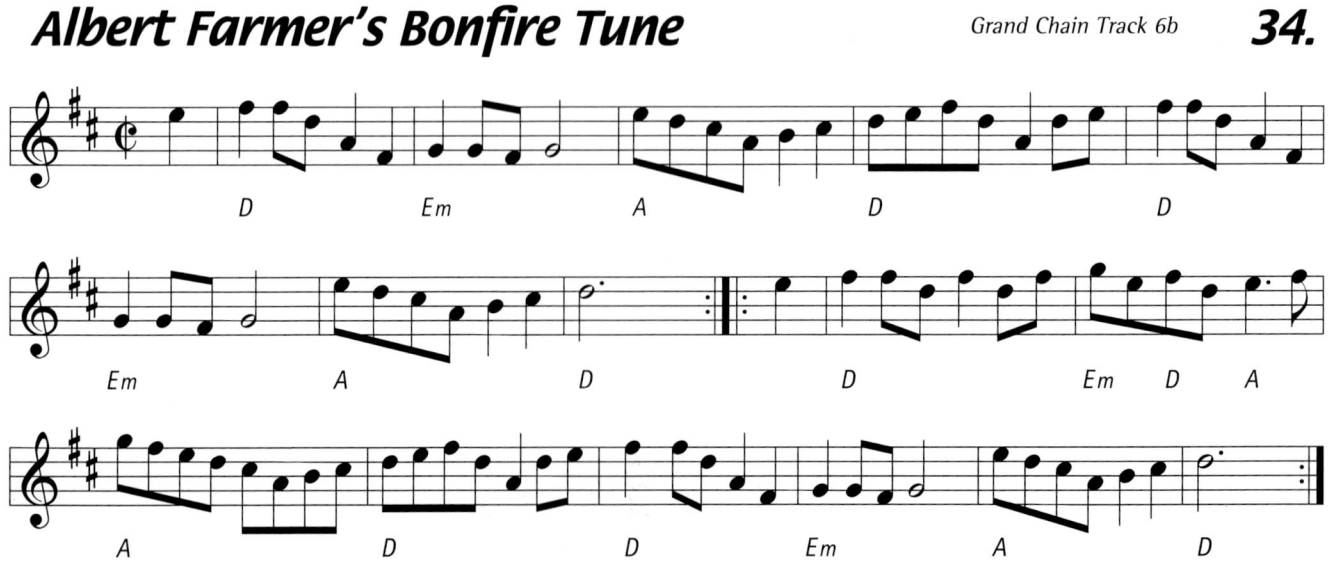

Albert Farmer's Bonfire Tune

Grand Chain Track 6b — **34.**

35. Watson's Hornpipe
Grand Chain Track 6c

WATSON'S HORNPIPE is a great tune and we have to thank the band Grand Union for popularising it.

GRAND CHAIN is probably of French-Canadian origin, and is also known as **La Grande Chaine**. It is very popular in the North-East of England.

36. Grand Chain
Grand Chain Track 7a

Nick Barber's English Selection

Hill's Fancy
Written by James Hill   Grand Chain Track 7b   **37.**

Some of James Hill's music is technically challenging - but HILL'S FANCY is very simple, while still having the driving rhythm that makes it a good session tune.

DOUBLE FIGURE EIGHT was recorded by the Old Swan Band, and is available in their compilation album, *Still Swanning after all these Years*, 1995. This is always a popular session tune.

WILL'S WAY was written by Will Ward - at the time playing bassoon with the band Fiddlers Dram.

SWEEPS HORNPIPE is from the manuscript of John Moore. Other tunes also use this title - including one which I would call **The Belfast Hornpipe**.

TOM TOLLEY'S HORNPIPE is also known as **Tom Fowler's Hornpipe**. There is a "short" version of this tune in circulation, which lacks the distinctive repeated notes of bars 13 and 14.

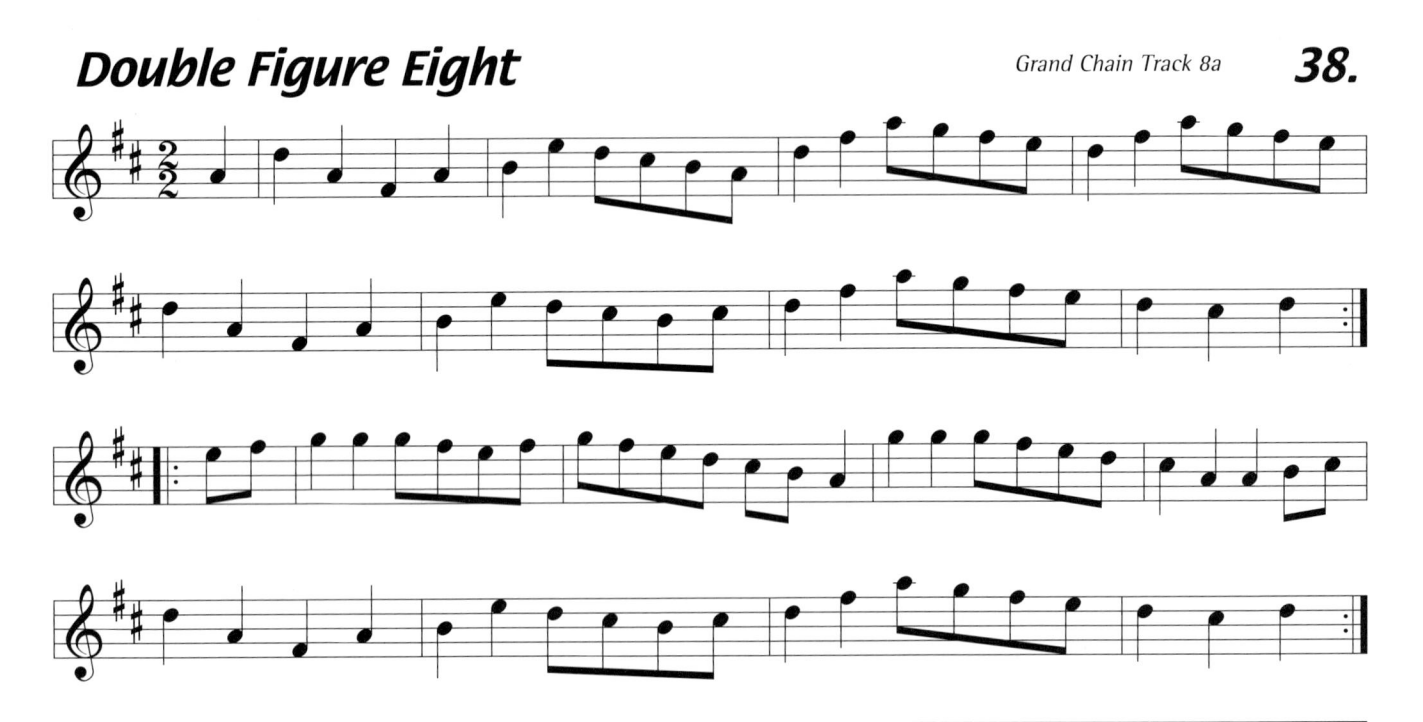

Double Figure Eight
Grand Chain Track 8a   **38.**

James Hill - The Lads Like Beer

James Hill was a prominent fiddle player and composer, living on Tyneside in the mid-nineteenth century. He was referred to by a contemporary as "the daddy of them all at hornpipe playing" and many of his tunes are still played in English sessions.

Graham Dixon's *The Lads Like Beer - The Fiddle Music of James Hill* is a good introduction to the man, his music, and the place of fiddle music in a Victorian urban community.

39. Grand Chain Track 8b Written by Will Ward **Will's Way**

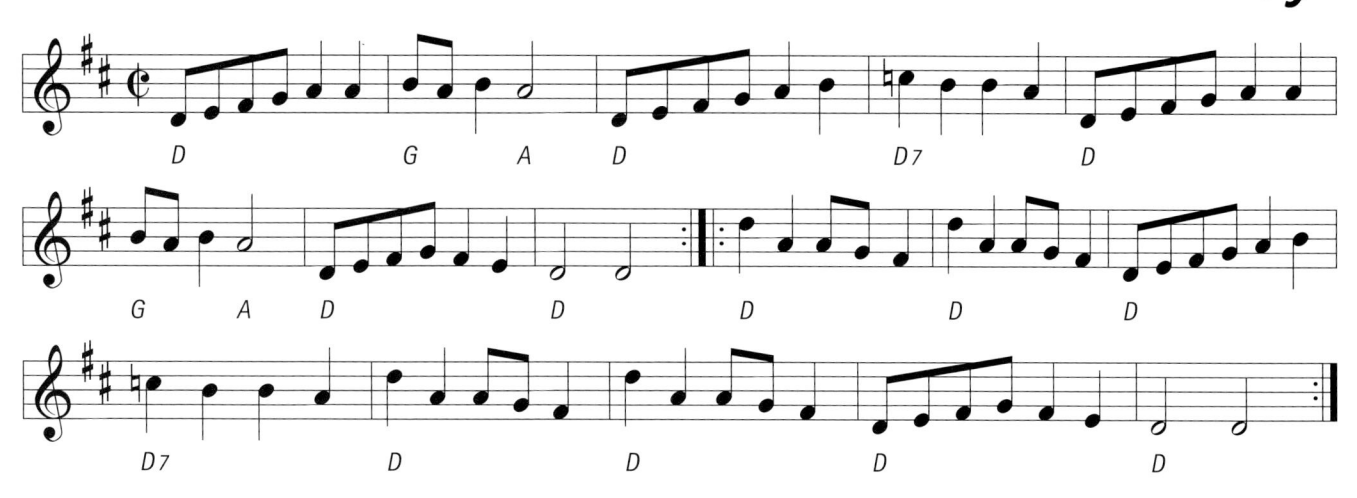

40. Grand Chain Track 9a **Sweeps Hornpipe**

41. Grand Chain Track 9b **Tom Tolley's Hornpipe**

Nick Barber's English Selection

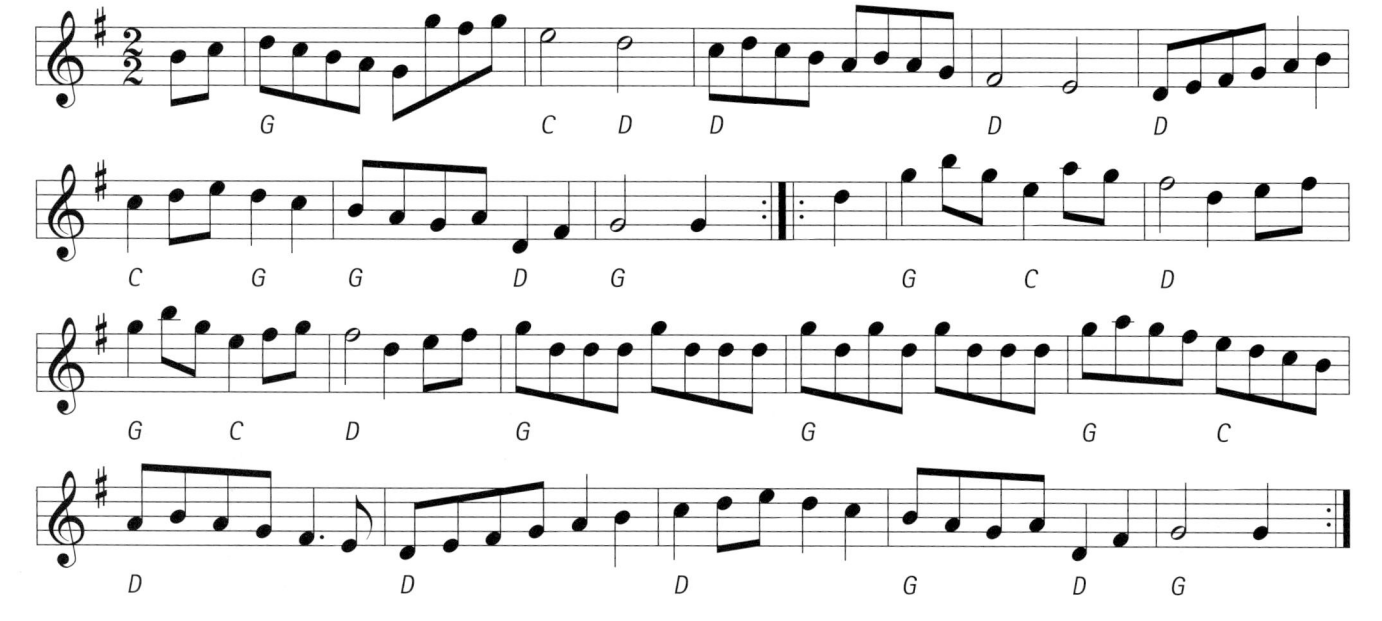

Little Burnt Potato

Written by Collin J. Boyd
Grand Chain Track 10
42.

[Sheet music in 6/8 with chords: G D G G D Am D / D D G D G / G G G D D / D D G D G]

LITTLE BURNT POTATO was composed by the Nova Scotian Collin J. Boyd, and became a fiddle players' favourite after being broadcast by Canadian fiddle player and TV personality Don Messer.

BASQUET OF OYSTERS was put together by Pete Coe from parts of a basque tune.

Basquet of Oysters

Grand Chain Track 11
43.

[Sheet music in 6/8 with chords: G D C G G D / C D C G Am D G / G C D G C G D / C G C G D C G]

22   Nick Barber's English Selection

Main Course

44. *Grand Chain Track 12* — ***The Valiant***

THE VALIANT was composed by Simon Ritchie - exponent of East Anglian song and step dance, and melodeon player for the Posh Band. The title relates to an old sailor who had been on the HMS Valiant during World War II.

TYSKEREN was learned from the playing of Danish melodeon player Carl Erik Lundgaard Jensen. It is an example of a range of old south German folk dance tunes known as *Zwiefacher*. This loosely translates as "two times".

45. *Grand Chain Track 13* — ***Tyskeren***

Poolside Polka
Written by Cliff Stapleton Grand Chain Track 14 **46.**

POOLSIDE POLKA was written by Cliff Stapleton, hurdy-gurdy player with Blowzabella and Stocai. It was written for two reasons - as English traditional music for a theatre show, and as a 48-bar polka for Blowzabella.

DENNINGTON BELL is from the playing of Dolly Curtis, whose family ran the pub in Dennington, The Bell. This pub was one of many Suffolk pubs where musicians gathered regularly. See *Before the night was out...* edited by Katie Howson.

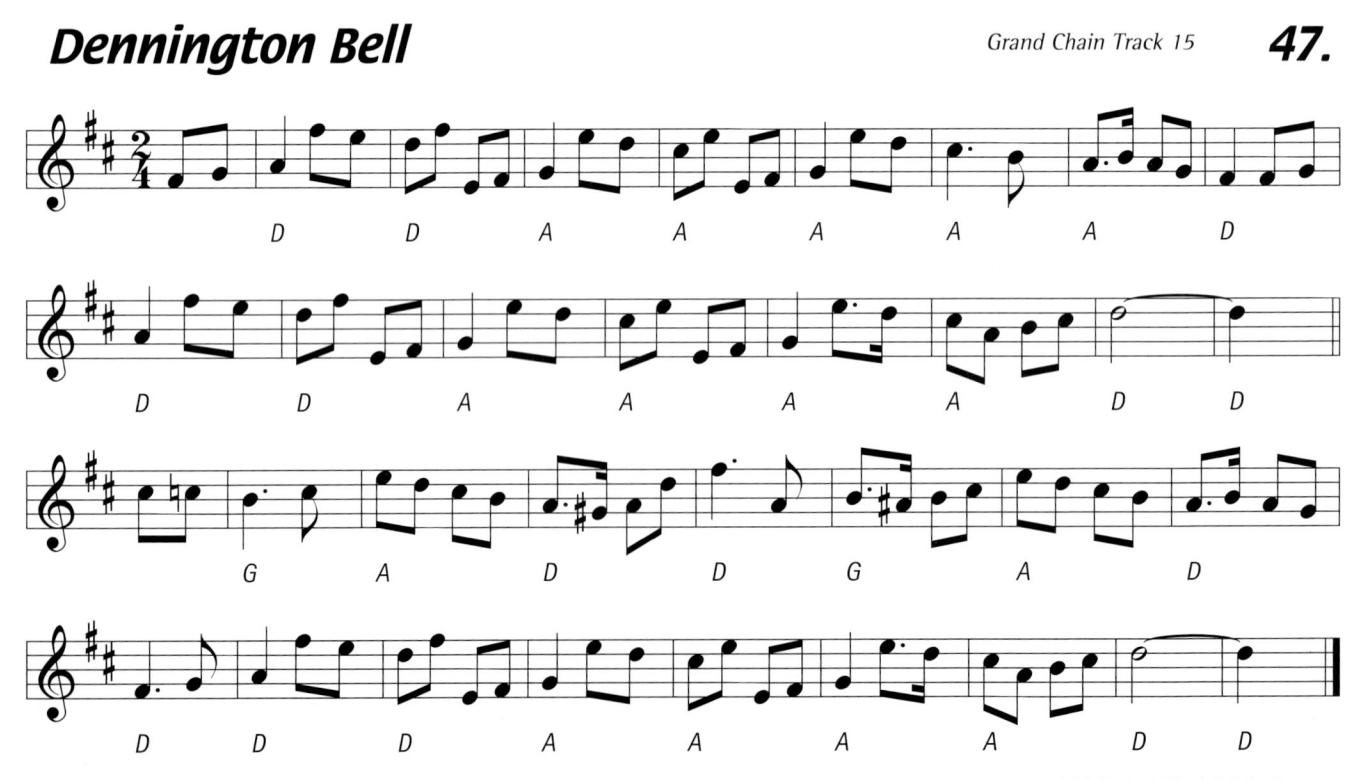

Dennington Bell
Grand Chain Track 15 **47.**

48. Bath Hornpipe
Grand Chain Track 16a

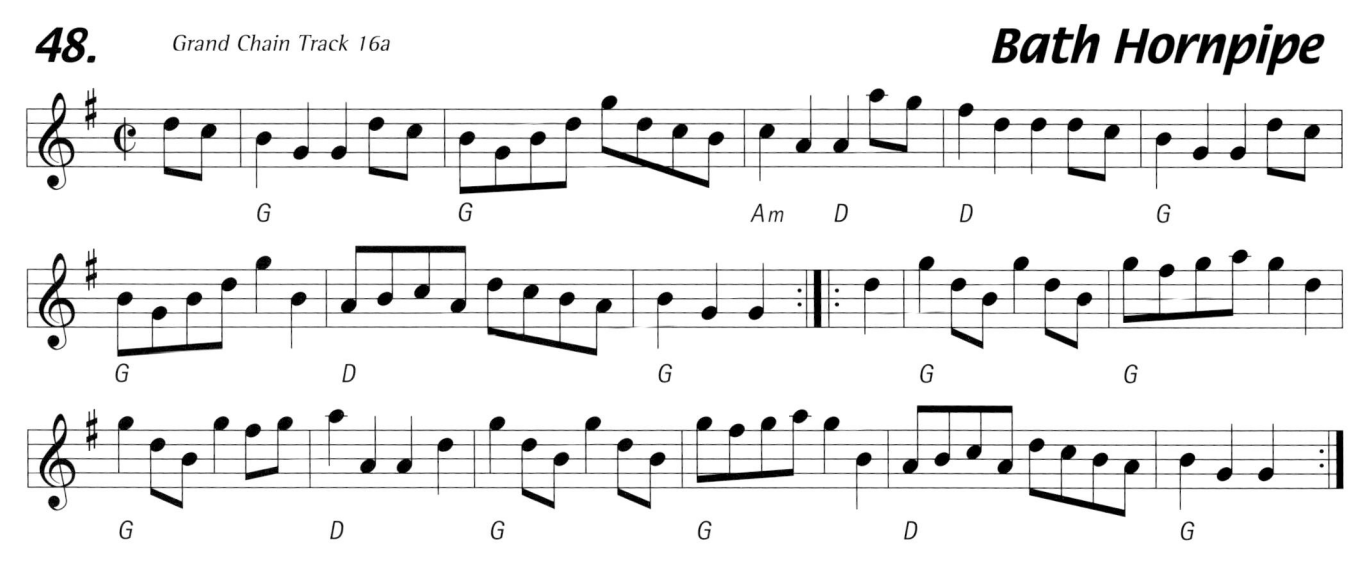

BATH HORNPIPE appears in *The Fiddler of Helperby* as **Untitled I**, as well as in Frank Kidson's *Hornpipes* of 1900. COOK HORNPIPE is a Yorkshire tune, appearing in the same two sources. Kidson notes that the tune was very popular with a small musical society in Leeds in the early 19th century, and calls it the **Kirkgate Hornpipe** after the Leeds street, Kirkgate, where they met.

There are a large number of variations of CUCKOO'S NEST. The version given here is close to that in *The Fiddler of Helperby*. It can be played as a dance tune, but it also goes well played quite slowly.

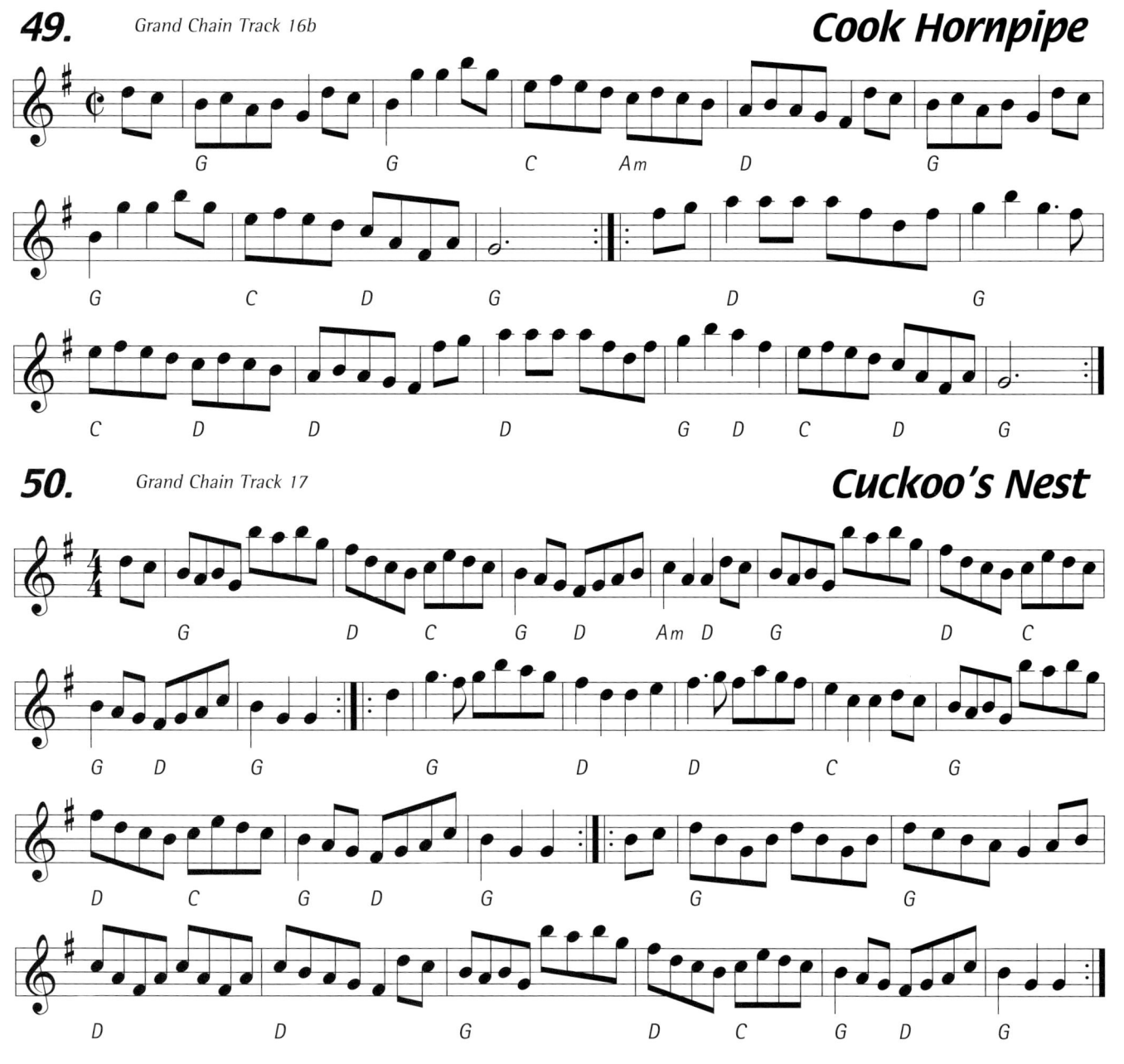

49. Cook Hornpipe
Grand Chain Track 16b

50. Cuckoo's Nest
Grand Chain Track 17

Nick Barber's English Selection

Miss Gayton's Hornpipe
Grand Chain Track 16c — **51.**

Miss Menager's Hornpipe
Grand Chain Track 18a — **52.**

Holywell Hornpipe
Grand Chain Track 18b — **53.**

Lawrence Leadley, the Fiddler of Helperby
The manuscript books of the nineteenth-century Yorkshire fiddle player Lawrence Leadley are available as *Lawrence Leadley - The Fiddler of Helperby* presented by James Merryweather and Matt Seattle. This book contains many fine tunes, not easily found elsewhere, as well as a wealth of historical and biographical detail.

54. Officer's Polka
Grand Chain Track 19a

Both Miss Gayton and Miss Menager (Mary Ménage) were dancers around the turn of the nineteenth century.
HOLYWELL HORNPIPE is another great Yorkshire tune from *The Fiddler of Helperby*.
OFFICER'S POLKA was recorded by Tufty Swift and Sue Harris (*How to Make a Bakewell Tart*).

MR REW'S POLKA was collected by Peter Kennedy from Willliam Rew of Sidbury, Devon.
CLEE HILL is from the mouth-organ playing of Dennis Crowther, a Shropshire singer, story-teller, poet, musician and all-round entertainer.

55. Mr Rew's Polka
Grand Chain Track 19b

56. Clee Hill
Grand Chain Track 19c

Nick Barber's English Selection

Roman Wall

Grand Chain Track 20a **57.**

ROMAN WALL is related to Irish tune **The Eavesdropper**.
EAST BOLDON is from the mid-nineteenth century manuscript tune book of William Lister of East Boldon - simply marked "No 28" and signed Robert Lister. This tune has been popularised by the playing of Pete Coe.

East Bolden

Grand Chain Track 20b **58.**

FARNE resources (http://www.asaplive.com/farne-home)
FARNE - the Folk Archive Resource North East - is a searchable online archive where you can find images of every page of a large number of manuscript tunebooks dating back to the seventeenth century. Included are collections from Henry Atkinson (1694/5), William Vickers (1770) and William Lister (1840-60), as well as many other tune books, song books and photograph collections. Also included are a number of interesting sound and video archives. The tune "East Bolden" was learned from the Lister Manuscript in this archive.

28   Nick Barber's English Selection

59. Ann Frazer McKenzie
Grand Chain Track 20c

60. Duke of York's Quickstep
Grand Chain Track 21

61. Boys of School Hill
Grand Chain Track 22

ANN FRAZER MCKENZIE is popular with Scottish fiddlers and this is a great dance tune!

DUKE OF YORK'S QUICKSTEP can be found in the Joshua Gibbons manuscript.

The origin of BOYS OF SCHOOL HILL, a version of "The Boys of Bluehill", is unclear. It has become known through the sessions at the Lewes Arms Folk Club, Lewes, Sussex.

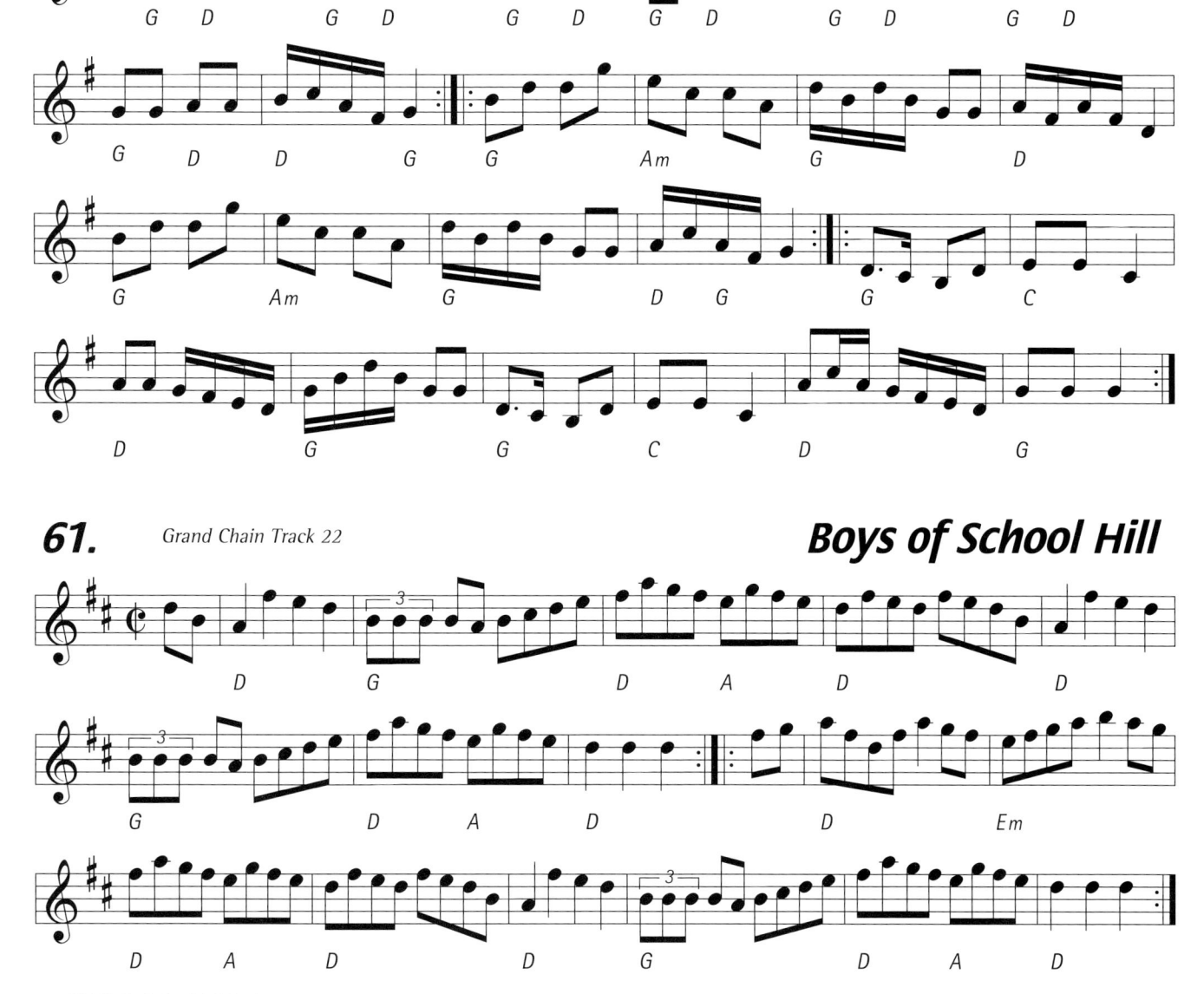

Nick Barber's English Selection

Mount Hills

Grand Chain Track 23a **62.**

MOUNT HILLS is from Playford's *Dancing Master*.
MAIDEN LANE is also from Playford.
BUS STOP was composed by Will Hampson at the age of 14 whilst waiting for the bus to school.

Maiden Lane

Grand Chain Track 23b **63.**

KURAKIN is from Hodsdull's *24 Favourite Country Dances for the Year 1826*. Not a well-known tune, but easy to pick up by ear.

Bus Stop

Grand Chain Track 24a **64.**

Kurakin

Grand Chain Track 24b **65.**

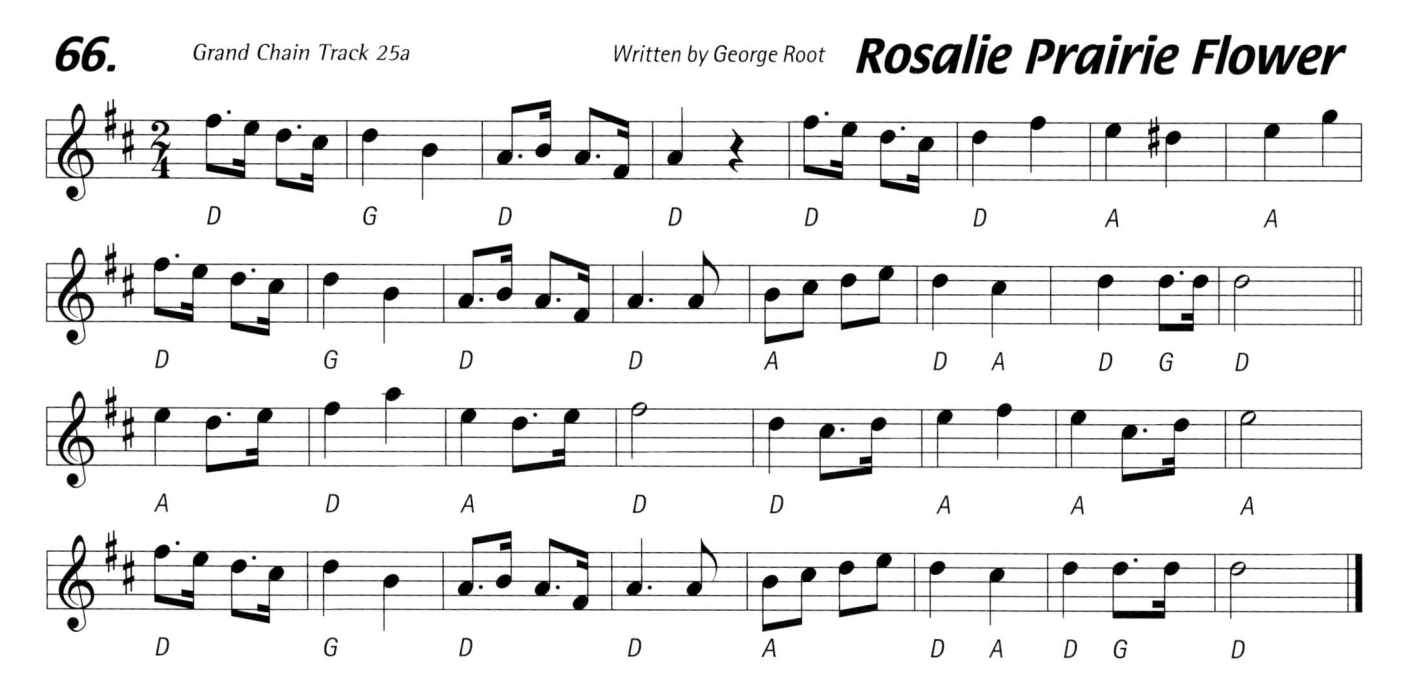

66. Rosalie Prairie Flower
Grand Chain Track 25a — Written by George Root

ROSALIE PRARIE FLOWER was composed in 1855 by American songwriter George Root, who became known during the American civil war with compositions including **The Battle Cry of Freedom** and **Tramp Tramp Tramp**.

KIRKGATE HORNPIPE is a very well-known hornpipe, but still one of the best!!

MARCH IN BLUEBEARD is from the enormously popular 19th century opera *Blue Beard, or Female Curiosity*. It is one of the earliest recorded folk tunes, found on a barrel organ recording used by Admiral Parry for a polar expedition in 1810.

67. Kirkgate Hornpipe
Grand Chain Track 25b

68. March in Bluebeard
Grand Chain Track 26

Nick Barber's English Selection

Shropshire Lass

Grand Chain Track 27 — **69.**

LNB Polka

Grand Chain Track 28 — **70.**

SHROPSHIRE LASS is a dance tune not found in *Playford's Dancing Master*, but in its successor of 1713 published by John Young. Walsh's *New Country Dancing Master, 2nd Book* of 1710 is the earliest source. This session version is slightly simpler than the published versions.

LNB POLKA was written by Alan Lamb and published in *Encyclopaedia Blowzabellica*. This tune has been taken up enthusiastically by a number border morris teams.

RADSTOCK JIG was collected by Cecil Sharp from the fiddler James Higgins, at 78 years old, living in Shepton Mallett workhouse at the time.

LEEDS POLKA is from the tune book *(Yorkshire Dance Tunes, 1900)* of Leeds folksong collector Frank Kidson.

GRAND HORNPIPE is from the Cumbrian manuscript of Henry Stables (1881). There is a very different "Grand Hornpipe" from Kentucky, also known as "Rocky Mountain Goat".

There are a few versions of FOURPENCE HALFPENNY FARTHING, with a variety of titles, including **The Jockey, Norickystie , The Wild Irishman**, and **Kiss'd Behind the Garden**.

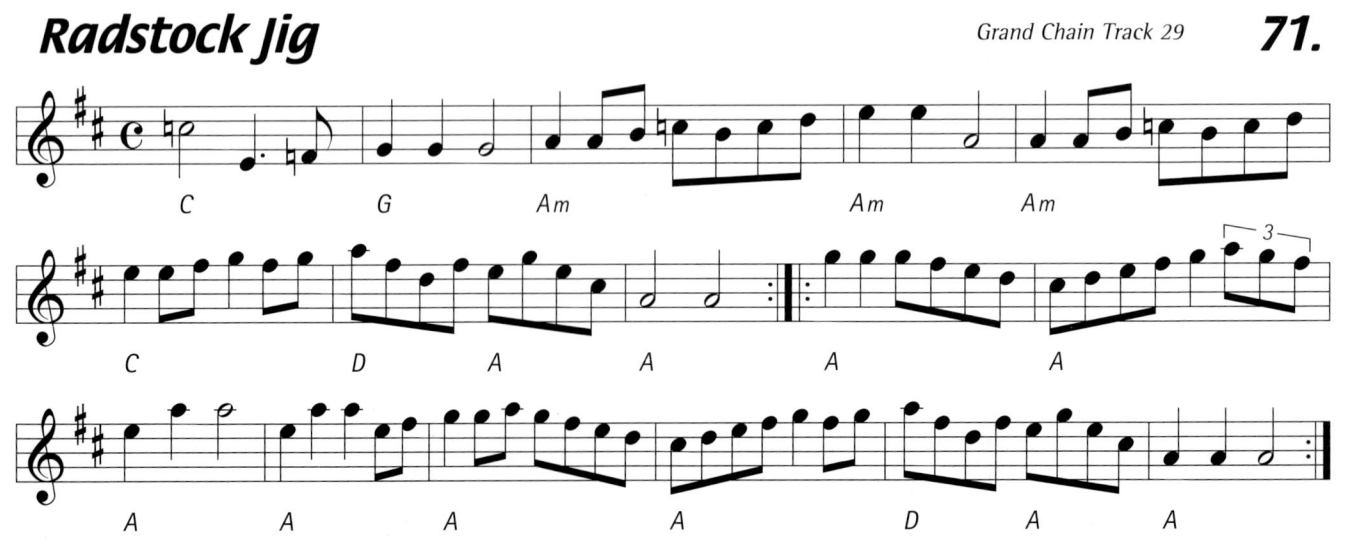

Radstock Jig

Grand Chain Track 29 — **71.**

72. Leeds Polka
Grand Chain Track 30

73. Grand Hornpipe
Grand Chain Track 31

74. Fourpence Halfpenny Farthing
Grand Chain Track 32a

The Flight

Grand Chain Track 33a **75.**

THE FLIGHT and THE BALL are two fine jigs from Thomas Hardy - though this version of THE BALL is a combination of that found in Hardy and that in *William Mittell His Book*. BELLINGHAM BOAT is a popular jig from the north-east of England, found in the Lister Manuscript, which is available online as part of the Folk Archive Resource North East (see page 28).

The Ball

Grand Chain Track 33b **76.**

Bellingham Boat

Grand Chain Track 32b **77.**

Dessert

78. Oldham Rant Track 12 — **Draper's Maggot**

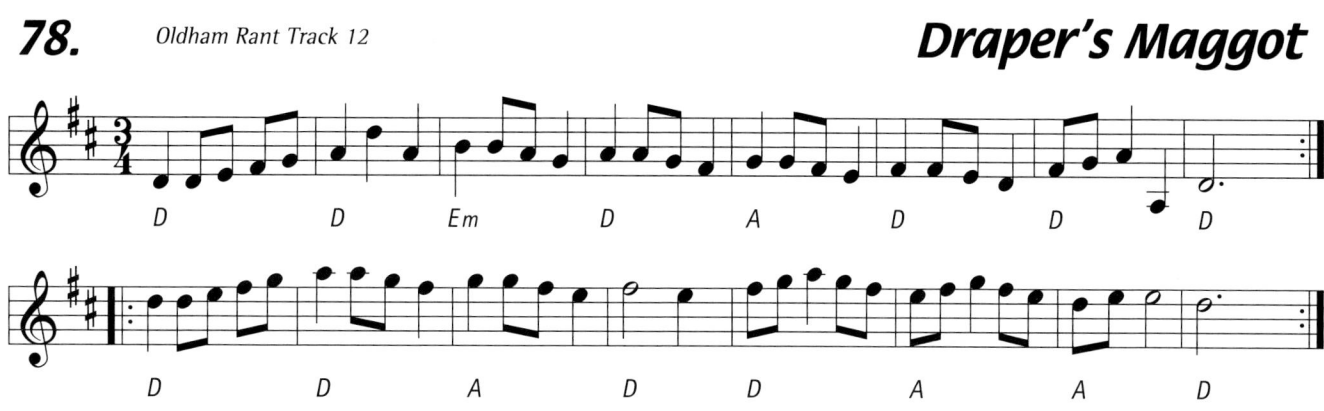

DRAPER'S MAGGOT is one of 19 "maggots" in Playford's *Dancing Master*. The word means a whim or a fancy, and does not refer to the creature found in decaying matter.

Like so many good tunes, BLOOMSBURY MARKET works played at a variety of speeds. Originally a dance tune from Playford's *Dancing Master*, it works well played quite slowly.

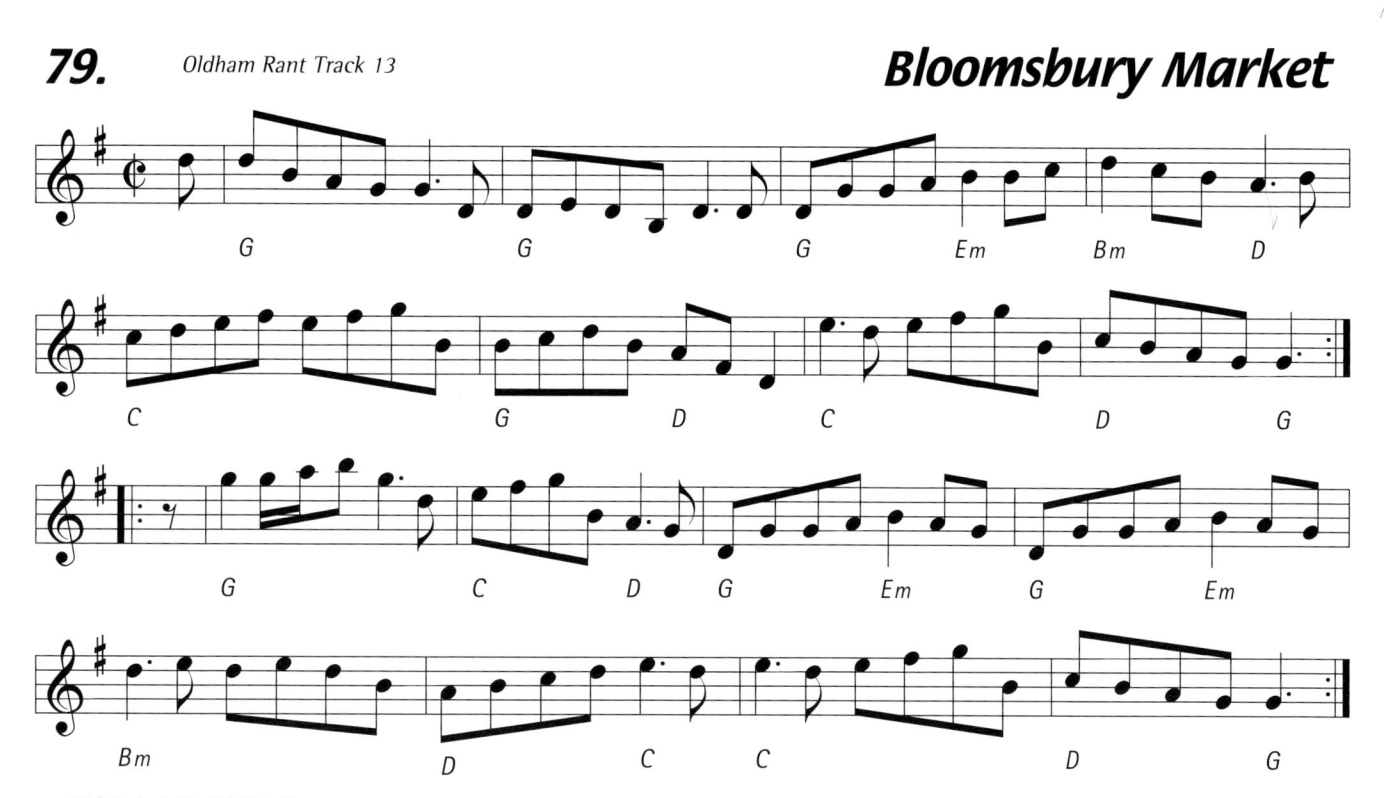

79. Oldham Rant Track 13 — **Bloomsbury Market**

Nick Barber's English Selection

Robertson's Hornpipe

Oldham Rant Track 14 — **80.**

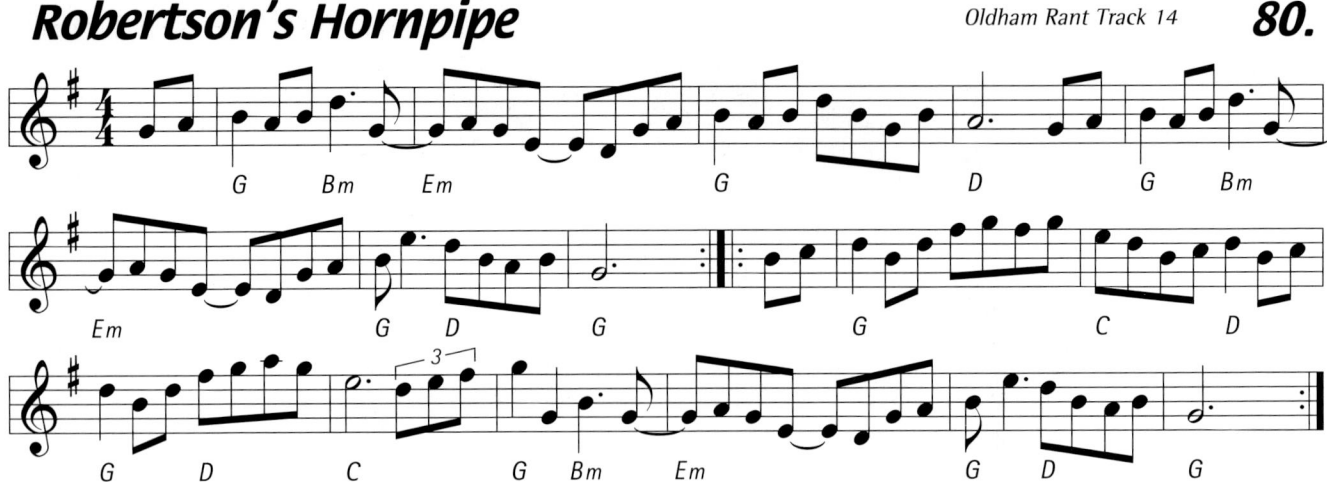

THE PLANE TREE and ROBERTSON'S HORNPIPE are examples of session musicians enjoying a game - playing a well-known tune in a new style. Make the most of the differences! This version of ROBERTSON'S HORNPIPE was the brain-child of Nigel Chippendale whilst playing with the band "Eric". Suddenly needing a step-hop tune, and being unable to immediately think of one, Nigel played this - and the band took to it immediately.

The Plane Tree

Oldham Rant Track 15 — **81.**

Said Too Much Already

Written by Nick Barber — *Oldham Rant Track 16a* — **82.**

Cumberland Waltz

Oldham Rant Track 16b — **83.**

Nick Barber's English Selection

84. L'Inconnue de Limoise
Oldham Rant Track 17

85. The Leaving of Lismore
Oldham Rant Track 18

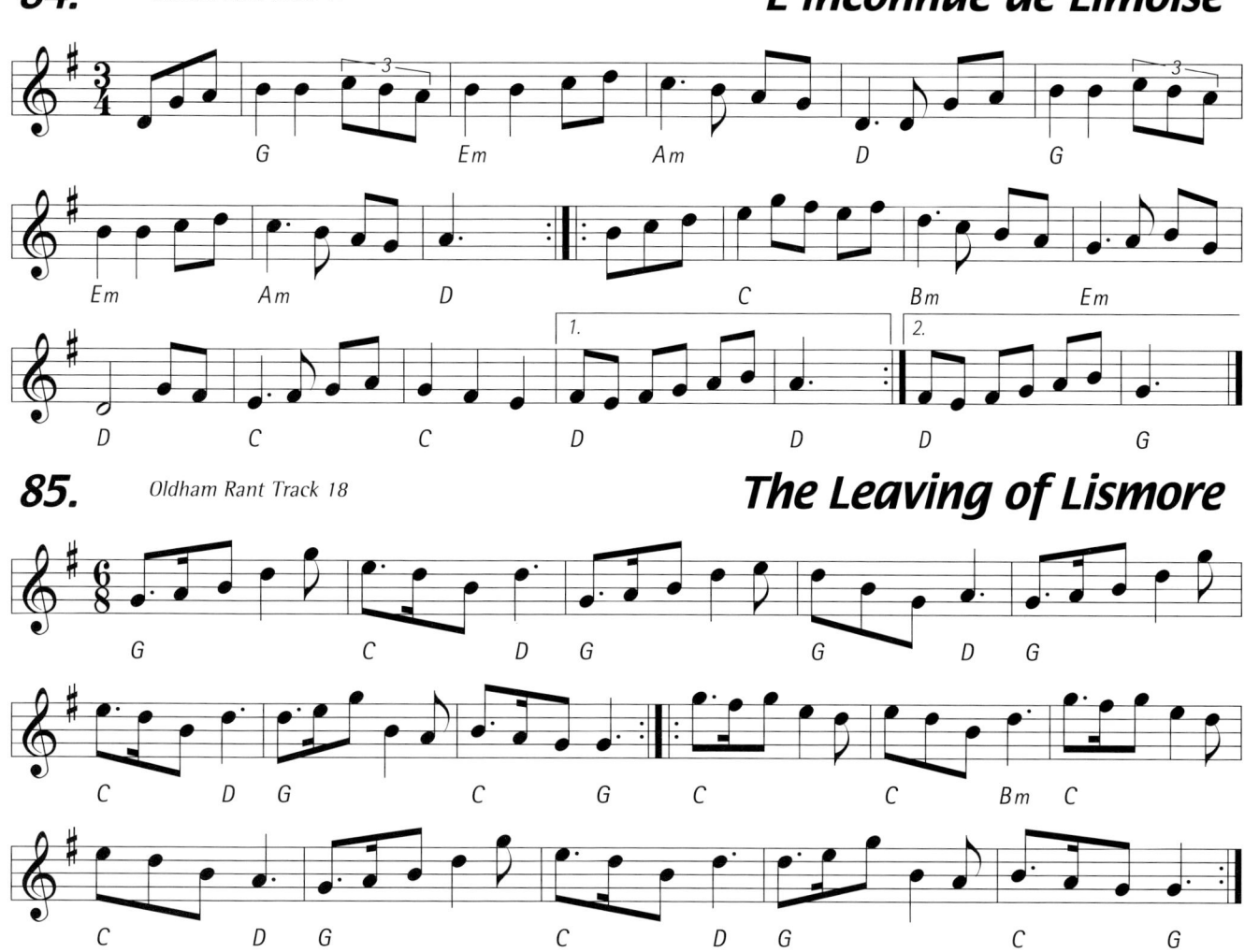

SAID TOO MUCH ALREADY was composed by Nick Barber in 1997, works well together with Wim Poesen's **Wals voor Polle** (see *Nick Barber's English Choice!*)

CUMBERLAND WALTZ was recorded on a barrel organ made by George Astor around 1810. This tune has become well-known since its publication in Jamie Knowles' *A Northern Lass*.

L'INCONNUE DE LIMOISE refers to an unknown piper whose skeleton and pipes were discovered in Limoise, prompting this tune from Maxou Heintzen.

THE LEAVING OF LISMORE is a Scottish pipe tune - which works well on other instruments. The Isle of Lismore lies in Loch Linnhe on the West Coast of Scotland.

JOUR D'ÉTÉ was composed by Frédérick Paris - see *Nick Barber's English Choice* for two more fine Paris compositions, **Le Canal en Octobre** and **Ganivelle**.

86. Jour d'Été
Oldham Rant Track 19 — Written by Frédérick Paris

Nick Barber's English Selection

Westmorland

Oldham Rant Track 20 **87.**

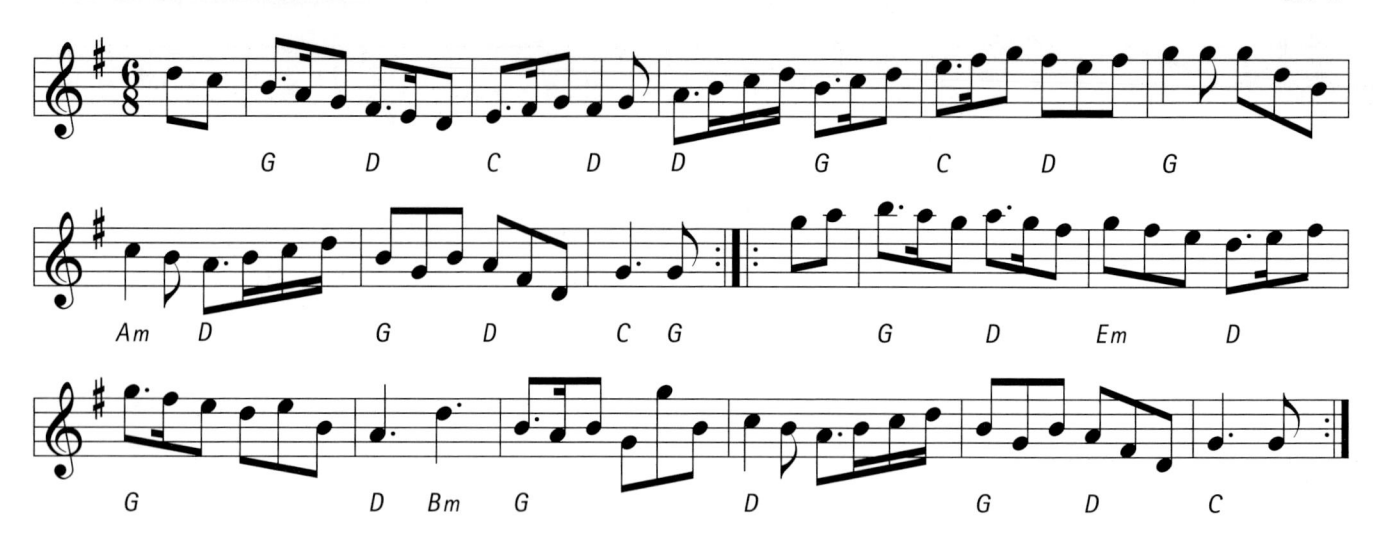

WESTMORLAND was written in 6/4 time, and probably intended as a jig. This tune also goes well as a waltz.
HOLE IN THE WALL is a lovely gentle dance tune from Playford's *English Dancing Master*.
FRENCH WALTZ is a wonderful waltz from the pen of Montreal melodeon maestro Philippe Bruneau.

Listening to IN THE TOYSHOP, you can hear the title in the music. This tune was found by Pete Rogan in a music library - on a fairground organ LP.
MICK'S TUNE was a great favourite of Mick Brooks.
SOUTH DOWNS was composed by Jim Harding - trying things out on the anglo concertina as he awaited the birth of his son, Joby.

Hole in the Wall

Oldham Rant Track 21 **88.**

French Waltz

Oldham Rant Track 22 **89.**

Nick Barber's English Selection

90. In the Toyshop
Oldham Rant Track 23

Reggish

Oldham Rant Track 26 — **93.**

Never Again
Written by Nick Barber

Oldham Rant Track 27a — **94.**

REGGISH - "Er det en Scottish? Er det en reggae? Nae! Hvad er det sa? Det er en Reggish!" ("Is it a schottische? Is it reggae? No! What is it then? It's a Reggish!!") A mix of reggae and Danish folk dance from Keld Norgaard Kristensen.
NEVER AGAIN was composed by Nick Barber.

ADIEU LES FILLES DE MON PAYS is a French slow march - which can be played after NEVER AGAIN.
Adieu les filles de mon village, Adieu les filles de mon pays,
Adieu le charmant voisinage, Adieu la douce compagnie,
C'est aujourd'hui que nous partons, allons-y voir nos maîtresses,
C'est aujourd'hui que nous partons, allons-y voir nos maîtresses.

Les Filles de mon Pays

Oldham Rant Track 27b — **95.**